DISCARDED Around the World in 30 Years

DISCARDED

Around the World in 30 Years

Life as a Cultural Anthropologist

Barbara Gallatin Anderson

Southern Methodist University

WAVELAND
PRESS, INC.
Prospect Heights, Illinois

For information about this book, write or call:
Waveland Press, Inc.
P.O. Box 400
Prospect Heights, Illinois 60070
(847) 634-0081

For Robin,
brave and true

Contents

PSYCHOLOGICAL ANTHROPOLOGY

GENDER AND ETHNICITY

ACHIEVING GROUP IDENTITY

ART AND ANTHROPOLOGY

THE CHALLENGE OF CHANGE

Prologue

Identification of oneself as an anthropologist triggers fairly predictable reactions. People at parties and strangers on planes will want to share with you memories of spectacular archeological sites, or they will have questions as to the validity of claims that the body of a woman found by a local roadwork crew is 12,000 years old. In this amiable inquisitiveness they share in the not uncommon conviction that anthropologists, by definition, move about the world unearthing things. Indiana Jones has a lot to answer for.

Where the immediate prospect is one of side-by-side togetherness on a ten-hour flight, a choice suggests itself to those of us who, as anthropologists, do not routinely dig nor focus on past cultures. Go along with their enthusiasms as best we can, short of misrepresentation, or launch into a few clarifications about the field of anthropology in general.

Yes, you are an anthropologist, but although anthropologists are broadly trained (digressions here can be lengthy), your field of specialization is neither archeology nor physical anthropology. You are a cultural anthropologist. In particular, an ethnologist. You work with live people, not dead ones.

Time and multiple plane trips, however, have left me less sanguine about identifying myself as an anthropologist at all.

1

It is simply no good trying to explain to a fellow passenger why you are traveling six thousand miles to a destination spurned by tourists, to watch and listen to men and women, every one of whom is a stranger to you, and none of whom will be keen about your presence among them. It would take less time to explain why you are a fleeing embezzler.

In villages, towns, and cities of the world cultural anthropologists seek out all kinds of people into whose worlds they must make entrance. They find themselves dependent on the goodwill—or minimally, approachability—of strangers in exploring the commonplace as well as more intimate, less-shared dimensions of daily life. This is *fieldwork*.

Doing fieldwork over long periods of time, both with empathy and with the monitoring dispassion of a trained observer, constitutes the insider/outsider duality of our discipline. In reporting on the ways of life of peoples of the world, cultural anthropologists involve themselves in the activities of their chosen communities. They keep "fieldnotes" on what they learn. And later, with the polish of post-fieldwork reflection, publish their best efforts. In regional and national conferences, anthropologists communicate with one another, inviting comparative debate. In the ideal course of things, insight into human behavior, its roots, complexity, and variation builds within anthropological literature—and sometimes beyond.

This is the course of wisdom. The reader needs to know, however, that not all cultural anthropologists find themselves unerringly on so commendable a course . . . as the following chapters will surely confirm.

Fortunately for me, a variety of opportunities and enticements have moved me about the world more widely than I had ever planned. This book draws upon some of the fieldwork involved. That the cumulative time span is far from negligible absolves me, I hope, from too sober judgment upon the diversity of cultures represented and the brevity of my treatment of them. No selective recall of a culture can prove as edifying as a full and proper ethnographic account of it. I know that. But my goal here is more modest and limited.

I have tried to take the reader along with me in terms of the impact and immediacy of fieldwork as it affects the anthropologist—at least *this* anthropologist.

I had three mandates for including a particular narrative: 1) it provided insight into a dimension of culture I might otherwise not have acquired; 2) it speaks to the inevitable failures as well as successes in fieldwork; and 3) it makes visible the anthropologist in the vulnerability of the field theater, in contexts different from published reports, with their selective hindsight.

This book documents encounters with various people's formulas or game plans for survival and getting along with one another, largely by virtue of having been born at a particular place, to a particular family, at a particular time in history.

Of sustained interest to me have been the cognitive and emotional profiles of the world's peoples to the extent that these can be captured. Minimally this involves not only a comprehension of wide-ranging formulas for living but an identification with and empathy for the logic that underlies them. An ambitious and often humbling effort.

Part of the challenge lies in recognizing the kind of "receptors" that we as anthropologists bring to the field: the learned codes within us for becoming involved in life around us, for processing and translating what we see and experience—meaningfully and justly.

Intellectually and emotionally (a contrived dichotomy!) the anthropologist walks a tightrope. Fieldwork classes prepare us for what to do, and that training is critical. What we can less adequately be prepared for is how we internalize the field experience, what each of us as anthropologists will draw upon in registering life around us. The "jigsaw" of our own lives, our relationships as sons and daughters, spouses or parents, our codes of behavior and judgment: these are "tamed" in the field but never rendered wholly inoperable. Indeed, we learn gradually to put them to use in identifying with the particular social "fit" that shapes a people's view of themselves, of family, of others, and of the world around them.

Anthropologists are cultural translators. Basically they find themselves projecting what, analytically at least, can be viewed as a multiple-personality approach to fieldwork. Behavior that might well invite psychiatric scrutiny at home becomes standard operating procedure in the field. This is because the acrobatics of fieldwork demand changing levels of readiness and newly adaptive behaviors on the part of the anthropologist. Put more simply, we learn to function from whatever reservoirs of "self" (more accurately of "selves"), from whatever assets of experience, empathy, or identification we can draw upon to make sense of unfamiliar worlds.

And we are actors.

Vicariously we "become" the local sons and daughters, wives and husbands, parents with children in tow, friends, neighbors, tradespeople and curers. The list is long. We register experience through these and other very personal lenses. We project, however formlessly, a new and varied identity within the field "theater." In terms of the *community*'s vision of *us*, we retain at best a suspect identity. Even the most gracious villagers and townspeople have difficulty advancing a plausible framework for our activity among them.

Essentially we are invaders . . . however discreet our hovering. Within the "niche" that people everywhere seek to assign us, we are the persistent *"stranger."*

Whatever the script, the irony of fieldwork lies in that compellingly unresolved insider/outsider challenge central to the most modest degree of success in work as a cultural anthropologist.

THE BASICS
Doing Anthropology

1

The Anthropologist as Listener and Observer
A French Farm Village

Fieldwork routinely subsumes a great deal of relatively commonplace activities—listening, observing, participating in life around us. In doing fieldwork anthropologists extend the context of years of academic training, much of which—ideally at least—will have related directly to the general geographic area selected for study. And once in the field we begin the slow travail of building insight, often in the context of particular questions about human behavior. Not uncommonly, however, few of the activities for which we have prepared ourselves will have an easy threshold.

Take the simple but requisite act of "listening."

Nothing brings home the reality of here-I-am-in-the-field faster than the plunge into a universe wherein the most taken-for-granted dimension of daily life—a shared language—is absent, or at best troublesome. Whatever the preparation for work in another language (in whose mastery one is routinely tested as a graduate student), "first days" in a community are a jungle of sound. People seem to speak with inordinate speed, enunciate badly, and rarely understand your best rehearsed overtures. And it can be months before one's brain gives up the clumsy practice of "translating" every word into English and devotes its energies less torturously to just plain *listening*. Admittedly, listening alone will not get anyone creditably through a field assignment. But listening skills are a far from modest part of the gamut of resources needed in the field. In the early days of finding one's way, setting up housekeeping, and making contacts, listening constitutes the cultural anthropologist's principal arsenal of adaptation together with another much underrated skill: *observing*.

Indeed, productive listening and observation lay the foundation for the higher goal of *participation* in the local culture with minimum trauma. This chapter deals essentially with the first two of these challenges, the next with the complexities of participation.

In my two-year study of French village life,[1] a woman to whom I listened regularly was Louise Paligny (a fictitious name). She was one of my "informants." *Informant* is a designation anthropologists use to refer to those few men and women on whom we come to depend for a significant amount of cultural insight. My comfort with the term has dwindled, and I rarely use it. Politically dangerous, it can convey an inappropriately sinister meaning. Casual reference to an informant will get you (*and* the informant) into trouble in many parts of today's world. And for some anthropologists the term *consultant* has proved a worthy substitute, as has *advisor*. I'm still searching.

The village of Vertier (a pseudonym) lies within fifteen miles of Paris, a closeness that historically had little meaning for most villagers. Even in the lifetime of 89-year-old Louise: "You would not know there was a world beyond." Buildings in the old quarter still looked much as they did when the peasants paid their grain taxes to a feudal lord and, through good harvests and bad, worked the land, married, and died largely unaffected by centuries of French history. The revolution of 1789, a momentous event on the national and international scene, created only a brief (although important) upheaval in local life.

But by the time of my visit the "world beyond" had come. It was irrevocably altering daily lives, gradually transforming Vertier from country village to Paris suburb. For many, the traditions of this small farm community endured. Yet, over the two-year period of my residence, the portrait assembled from village records and in-depth studies of villagers was of a community that had survived famines and wars but now faced intractable change.

Vertier had become an anachronism, even to itself, as tract homes intruded on ancient gray-walled streets. From an anthropological perspective, the behavior of its men and women in the face of these changes had relevance for the understanding of a process that—in one fashion or another—is occurring in peasant villages in much of today's world.

I went in search of Louise's flat in the old quarter, walking twice past the courtyard before finding it. The entrance was obscured by clotheslines hung deeply with bed linens and men's blue work clothes. Five houses, one larger than the rest, pressed together to form a "U" opening to the street. The cobblestoned border was cracked and patchy, and yellow *pissenlits* and weeds grew unevenly in the dirt seams. In front of the largest shuttered house was a planter of red geraniums. I could hear water running further up the street where a workman was scrubbing out the public clothes-washing pond.

My coming had not been unobserved, and as I climbed the two stairs in front of Number 9 the door opened before I could find a knocker or a bell.

My fluency in French was a product of the fortuitous opportunity, as a child, to attend a French school in San Francisco where, I remember, we sang "The Star Spangled Banner" before classes began and "The Marseillaise" when the day ended—and before being shepherded aboard buses whose swift and safe home delivery had enticed my parents to enroll me.

Now, in Vertier, it would be weeks before I got over the unimaginable joy of not facing a brand-new field language as I had had to do in my first fieldwork on a Danish island. The village-French, however, had a new tonality and now, facing my first real interview, I was ready for some heavy *listening*.

"Securité Sociale?"

The woman who had opened the door to me was in her thirties. She was wearing a *tablier*, a dress-length smock of muted plaid, lifelessly designed to obscure dirt and grease marks. We were in a long, low-ceilinged stone corridor with four doors of heavy unvarnished wood. These were a series of small flats.

Social Security workers, then ubiquitous in France, evoked mixed reactions, the most pervasive of which, in a village, was suspicion.

"No," I said. "Monsieur Bergerac from the post office directed me here. I would like to speak with Madame Paligny . . . if she is not resting."

I thought she had misunderstood me, for she walked past me into the courtyard but in an instant was back again. She pointed to a door facing hers. She and Madame Paligny had the choice front units with windows opening onto the courtyard.

I rapped several times with my knuckles against the heavy door.

"You will be there all day, my poor woman." She opened Madame Paligny's door, calling as she did. "Louise! —Ah! She is in the kitchen."

We were in an almost square room, perhaps fifteen by twenty feet, sunlit and full of the smell of wood and mold. It gave an impression of casual order that was characteristic of old-quarter residences. One did what one could in the face of housework: "On fait son possible." Literally, *one does one's possible* . . . beyond which there is only inner turmoil to be gained in overscrupulousness about conditions one cannot remedy.

Madame Paligny pushed aside a fringed brown drapery that curtained the rear kitchen area and appeared. The drapery fell into place behind her, and I could see the pronounced sag along one side where her hand must always have pushed at it.

"Michele!" she said, greeting her neighbor. Then she turned to me and nodded her head with slow and deliberate courtesy. I gave my name and extended my hand, but she smiled and quickly buried hers in her apron, elevating her wrist in an awkward gesture to touch my fingertips so that I should not think she spurned me. "I regret very much, but I have been preparing my little fish for dinner." She was tiny and deeply wrinkled.

"This lady is here from Pierre Bergerac to see you," Michele offered. "How are you, grandmother?"[2]

"Very well." She turned to me.

"I have come to speak with you because I . . ."

"Mesdames," the neighbor said, interrupting with this formal expression of leave-taking. "I'll see you, Louise." And she left, noiselessly closing the thick door.

I explained why my anthropologist husband and I had come with our two small children to study village life.

"Oh, but you have come too late!" Louise interjected. "That is all gone now. When I was a girl, yes, but now . . . the village has changed so." She was silent a moment. When I did not speak she said at last: "Do you think you could take that chair and put it next to mine . . . there, by the window?"

Alongside the bed was a straight-backed wooden chair, its seat padded with a round of patent leather, cracked and with white spots where the brown finish had been rubbed smooth. This was Madame Paligny's bedroom–sitting room. Opposite the window, against the curtained wall from which she had entered, was the bed. It had a tan woven spread that rose from the foot to a peak of pillows piled almost as high as the twin knobs that topped the bedpost. From one of these a length of string led in a low arc to the light fixture, where it attached to a chain. Beside the bed on a marble-top stand was a vast collection of medicine bottles, a glass and a spoon, some letters in their envelopes propped against a statue of Mary, and several folded squares of cloth. Along one wall were two chests of dark wood, side by side, and above them on the wall perhaps ten framed photos, largely of seated groups or children. Tacked alongside was a colorful picture of Our Lady of Perpetual Help that had been cut from a magazine. A calendar suspended by a red cord hung from a nail, and on one chest was a box of breakfast chocolate.

The curtains were beige, of wide netting with a cherub design worked into the base, an angel kneeling with arched bow in hand. These barely obscured the window and the black wrought-iron bar a foot above the sill, against which the shutters would close. In front of the window was the table beside which we were to sit. On it was her string shopping bag with the green tails of leeks sticking out and the familiar twisted package that almost surely identified a small cheese wedge.

I was to see the room many times, the unrelieved monochromes of floors and fabrics, the wallpaper a swirling faded pattern of beige and browns with white chalk bleeding through from the walls, and the peculiar musty odor of paste and mildew that was there even when the windows were wide open, as they were that first day.

She would not be seated until I had sat down.

"It is not like it used to be. No, not even in the *quartier*."

We talked for a little while. She spoke only in answer to my questions and with great cordiality despite the apparent uneasiness. The interview went a little stiffly.

After about fifteen minutes Madame Paligny had a visitor to whom I was introduced.

"This is Madame Beauchamps. She is very faithful and comes every day to talk with me and give me the news."

I had recognized Madame Beauchamps. She was a very large woman in a black dress that came to her ankles. Around her shoulders was a black scarf that tied under her chin. Even by the most indulgent villagers she was regarded as a character. She was said to live in one of the old courtyards near the *mairie*, in a room that no one had entered in the memory of the villagers. Reputedly it was a kind of depot for her collection of string and rags and old newspapers, but this was hearsay. She was unkempt and children were mildly afraid of her. Her day was spent visiting the old women of the village, and she gathered and dispensed along a limited circuit, news of the old quarter. She knew about me.

"You are the American lady for whom Madame Cluny works."

"Ah," said Madame Paligny, "I did not think of you as being that person . . . but, of course." She was pleased, I could see. I had a place in the scheme of things. If I was not truly "of the village," I had now at least a label affixed and was consequently less suspect. My association with things scientific, although disadvantageous in its vagueness, had healthy and commendable overtones.

"I was in service myself," she said, with the first show of enthusiasm, referring to my housekeeper now. "But that was in the old days. Oh yes, for many years. And my mother before me. Now, of course . . ." She spread her hands out, palms up, and at the same time thrust forward her chin, pursing her lips and audibly expelling air in a smacking sound, a village gesture of futility. "And lately, too, I could mend in the homes of the farm families, but my eyes are not good now."

After a few amenities I left, having made an appointment to come the next day, after Madame Paligny's nap, when I would escape her friend. I wondered what she would have to say about me.

In the course of a dozen or more visits Louise Paligny told of her life in Vertier. She was not strong and tired quickly. But maintaining continuity in our discussions was not as difficult as I expected. She asked to know in advance what we were to speak of so that she could reflect a little, a proposal to which I immediately regretted having agreed; I was afraid the arrangement would tempt her inordinately to invent the data I was seeking. She proved, however, not at all susceptible.

"I cannot remember. It is a shame, I know, but it has gone out of my mind." Sometimes when I pressed her a little, she would look at me with disappointment. "You do not want me to say what I do not know, I am sure. Perhaps Madame Charpentier... although I do not think so."

Madame Charpentier, at 91, was two years older than Louise and Vertier's oldest resident... but *not* a native. Eventually Louise had forgiven me for confusing the distinction and crediting Madame Charpentier with the honor so rightly hers, but she could occasionally not resist suggesting the comparative disadvantage and limitations of relying upon the recollections of a woman who had come to the village *only* as a bride of seventeen.

My reply, which instantly reassured her, was: "I don't think so either."

Reassembled over the weeks of our dialogue, with some inevitable gaps and a little lopsided now and then with the remembered highlights of ninety years of living, was a cultural framework of our joint construction.

Louise brought dead Vertier back to life: from her childhood as the only girl in a family of six children, all of whom lived to adulthood, through her courtship and marriage to a local farmer and the birth of her own two children (one of whom died in war), to her grandchildren and now great-grandchildren—whose world was so different from the world of farms that she had known. Yet her grandchildren lived close enough to visit often in a smart new Peugeot.

"And they are very good to me," she wanted me to know. "I could live with them if I wanted... but what should I do there without the things I know. Live outside the village (literally "mon pays"—my country)!!

"It is true I do not do much here now. But I have my 'rounds.' That is what the doctor says when he teases. And it is true enough. In the morning I go to Mass. When you are my age, it is the better part of wisdom—there is everything to gain. I go to the bakery and get a hot loaf. They cut a portion of the *batard* (a short French bread) for me because my teeth are almost gone and the crust is too hard in the *ficelle* (the most popular bread in the village and not much thicker than a fat breadstick). But dipped in coffee I like it better. Madame Gris gets my milk from the farm for which I pay each week, when she will take it. I do not drink much, that is true, but I cannot have my breakfast coffee without it.

"My little house is quickly in order, and once in a while Marie Claire (another neighbor) turns it inside-out for me. Then, morning and afternoon, a little nap. Not much in the morning, just enough to rest my feet before I go to buy my lunch makings. I have never neglected a good hot meal at noontime. It is easy to do that when one is alone, but without it where should my strength come from? . . . A bit of wine—the doctor has not forbidden me that.

"Last week I had a small spell and I was sick to my stomach at night and the doctor came. It was *grippe*. There is a lot of it in the village.

"In the afternoon I sit by the window and read the newspaper. When it is pleasant, Michele moves my chair out for me. I don't sew as I used to. At my age there is no use to protest.

"When I am asked, I go to the marriages and baptisms. That is not so often as before. It used to be that when the bells rang for a special event, you were already in the church or on the way. Now I hear them and sometimes wonder what it is for. The funerals, of course, you almost always know about. If not by mail, you see the announcement posted in the bakery windows.

"It used to be that every child who passed me on the street would greet me and wish me good day. I do not know whether they are less polite today or they do not know me. But, regardless, my mother would have given it to me soundly, I can tell you, for racing past as they do now without looking. However . . . it is the way things are.

"The old priest used to come by at least once a week. That was before your time. This one I never see. They say he has a television and does not go out. I don't know. There are always those who talk. Why should he come? The church is there. I was baptized there, received my First Communion there, married there, and when my day comes they will take me there.

"Until then I am content . . . I could have picked a worse place to be born."

Segmentation of ongoing fieldwork into ostensibly independent activities (listening, observing, participant observation) does violence to life as the cultural anthropologist experiences it anywhere in the world. I'm aware of that. Besides, when we get back to our universities and colleges to report on what we've done, the multiple sources of field data meld in ways that shape *new* reservoirs of insight—much of which we would be at serious pains to assign in terms of genesis.

Yet certain considerations, however intertwined, have been at the core of every field experience I've known.

When I interviewed Louise Paligny, I gave her my attention as she spoke or moved about, but principally I *listened*, taking notes as casually as I could manage. My French villagers were leery of recording devices of any kind, distrusting the "real purpose" involved in dragging these instruments into the privacy of homes or places of business. Notebook, pen or pencil were least likely to elevate what was already a marginal level of acceptance—even after two years in the community.

I also observed Louise. Had I the talent, I could sketch her still, from memory. I see her room, the walls and cabinets and effects of changing light on her face. As she became more used to my presence, she would get up from time to time, put on water for coffee, straighten a curtain, or she would lift a hand to her hair and reset the bone comb that held secure a large chignon above her neck. She shunned the use of her cane but checked periodically to be sure it was somewhere near. Louise animated much of Vertier's history for me.

The overriding purpose of my presence in her flat was the reconstruction of the village's *past* through her living of it, to comprehend the foundations out of which current village life had taken shape. To take that muted vision of Vertier's world into the "now" I needed to extend the canvas.

And one of the most engaging places for that was Jacqueline's Café where, principally, I *observed* (and, of course, listened).

Jacqueline's Café lay on Rue General Leclerc, the heart of "old town." Beyond it spread the multiplying villas of commuters whose daily world of work was in the process of revolutionizing local life. Within a hundred feet of the café lay the town hall, the public baths, weekend theater, firehouse and the post office. Most of Vertier's stores could be found on one side or the other of the continuous street that threaded its way from the "modern" pharmacy to a Familistère chain store displaying fresh produce, wines and cheese, a small collection of canned goods, beach sandals, some clothes and toys.

Jacqueline's was the smallest of Vertier's several cafés. Its ambiance pumped a sense of life into a village that was rarely gregarious and often reticent about the most casual dimensions of social intercourse. Jacqueline's was a gossip center . . . a disperser of local news and rumors.

Eventually, after almost a year's residence in Vertier, my presence in the café made little impact. I too was a "regular."

I had got on well with Jacqueline; although, like most of the villagers, she remained uncertain about what I was *doing* in Vertier. Little by little, however, her attitude toward me progressed from obvious discomfort about my eccentric interests to acceptance of the scientific overtones that clung (however inexplicably) to whatever I was doing. The consensus was that I was writing a history of the place.

Wine was the café's most popular drink, sold by the glass, red for the men and white usually for a comparative minority of women who found in "Madame Jacqueline's" a comfortable retreat. There were two entrances, one from the street and one from the adjoining minuscule grocery, which Jacqueline also owned and ran. Ladies might shop and then gracefully assuage their thirst at the bar without declaring it to the general community. It was a question of good taste, not of clandestine drinking, since the regular clientele was known to one another and their roster familiar to the villagers. At the time of my residence the women were principally middle-aged domestics, or shop and factory workers, many returning to their homes from Paris.

At noon, farmers and fieldhands and manual workers stopped by for a hot lunch. Each day of the week a different dish was featured. The Wednesday casserole of tripe and potatoes was magnificently fragrant, and on Fridays there were high, moist omelettes of mushrooms or cheese which, with French bread and a full-bodied wine, made up the inexpensive sumptuous fare that villagers took to be their prerogative as customers. Moderate business gave way to more brisk activity at the end of the workday.

Jacqueline was an ample woman of fifty. In the opinion of many she would not be indisposed to taking a third husband. Why else should she tolerate the tight corset she wore even in the heat of summer, or concern herself so scrupulously with grooming or dyeing her hair? The reddish-brown curls were set regularly—though it meant a bus ride to an evening appointment at the hairdresser's in Antony, the neighboring town. A good-looking woman, Jacqueline was shrewd at her work, but well liked by her clientele.

However, on one afternoon as I sat transcribing notes at a small rear table, Jacqueline was petulant. Blanche, the domestic, had arrived late for work, announcing as well that she was not coming in the next day. Her husband was sick again and she must go with him for X-rays.

"I had to cancel my appointment at Antony," Jacqueline whispered to me with a thrust of her head toward the kitchen where Blanche was washing the mountain of lunch dishes. "She has got herself a handful with that man." A shrug of the shoulders. "One never knows. Marriage is a lottery. My first husband . . . how he could spend money if I let him. Unfortunately he was not so adept at making it. A man to be rid of! My second, God rest him, left me all this . . . You take a chance."

A workman entered from the street in his work blues. He stumbled on the single step and to steady himself put out a hand to the window, painted halfway up in the familiar diamond pattern of blues and greens.

"The step is badly placed and if I should break a bone?" There was no rancor in his voice.

"I know this one very well," whispered Jacqueline. "Claude. It goes badly like every Friday." She jerked her hand to her mouth, mimicking a swiftly downed drink.

There was another man in the café, modestly dressed, but not in blues. The workman greeted him: "Monsieur." And, repeating the same two notes of rising inflection: "Mesdames!" His eyes went to Jacqueline and me. It was not expected that anyone reply. The greetings were customary on entering any publicly shared space.

Jacqueline poured red wine into a stem glass and placed it before the workman at the bar.

"I am tired," he said.

"Of doing nothing," said Jacqueline flatly.

"But no, Madame. I make my living." He tugged at the collar of his work shirt.

Blanche emerged from the back. With a small gesture of dismissal toward the workman, Jacqueline asked Blanche about her husband. The girl told her he was really bad yesterday. Dizzy. After she'd disappeared again, a second man approached the bar. Jacqueline filled his glass.

"He is only twenty-six," she volunteered to me, nodding toward the kitchen.

"She'll have no money." It came from the new customer.

"His mother has money." Jacqueline rubbed thumb and the tip of her index finger together in a gesture of affluence. The drunk straightened suddenly. "I am not afraid of work!"

"Sh-h. This is the café of silence." And, in an aside to me: "His family is from the north. They know how to drink there." Her lips formed the words carefully, her voice barely audible.

From the grocery entrance to the café a middle-aged woman, neatly dressed, came in and bought a glass of white wine, standing at the bar to talk with Jacqueline.

"How is it you are back so early?" Jacqueline probed. "Didn't you go to Antony?"

"I went all the way to Paris. What a trip! But what are you to do if you want good fabric? There was nothing, nothing, I tell you, in Antony. In ten minutes I found it at Mille Tissus. And at three o'clock it was already a brawl in the Metro, but I got an express. Thank goodness—I would be there still."

There was a snuffling sound as Madame Jacqueline's dog stretched and turned around in front of the potbellied stove. The newcomer turned and spoke to him in a cajoling, affectionate tone: "Kiki, Kiki, you are a faithful one. You do not play around." She turned to Jacqueline, leaning over the bar, her voice only slightly lowered.

"Did you hear them quarreling last night? They were in a state, I can tell you. And one wants only to be left in peace. I had to knock on the wall." She gestured with her thumb to the units above the bar where Jacqueline, I knew, rented small apartments.

"Ah, yes . . . I just saw her in the grocery. Her eyes were puffy, but she said nothing. And, of course, I am not one to inquire."

More quiet talking.

"But you know him," offered the woman. "He has always been wild."

"His brother, yes, but not Maurice. It is his *copains* (his buddies). They have changed him. He spends too much time in Paris."

"I did not raise mine like that, thank God."

"To have to knock on the walls," said Jacqueline, warming to her indignation. "One does not behave like that in Vertier."

The drunk said suddenly: "I go to church on Sunday!"

"You are not afraid it will fall on your head?" The woman had turned to look at him after a telling shrug from Jacqueline. "I do not go myself."

The man stood up, his hand in his pocket.

"How much?"

Jacqueline told him.

"Oh . . . give me another glass."

She poured the drink. "You pay now. That way we understand one another, eh?"

He tossed a bill on the bar, lifted the glass petulantly and swallowed the wine in a gulp.

"Monsieur . . . 'Dames." And he was gone.

"He is always cross, that one," said Jacqueline. "At night it is worse. His wife puts him out when he is bad. Poor beast. He sleeps in Henri's barn. He is not wicked. Just a poor devil of a little farmer."

The other woman turned to the gentleman who had silently witnessed all this and who now wanted to buy her a drink.

"One glass of white is all I take . . . but, if you insist. Today . . . I must admit! . . . And one is no longer twenty." She nodded, laughed, and Jacqueline poured the drink. In a few minutes the man left.

"There . . . there is a gentleman," said the woman, with the repeated head nodding that in the village was a gesture of profound commitment to one's statement.

When the woman, in turn, had left, a second came in, again from the grocery, with a brown parcel under her arm.

"Have the men gone? Zut! I thought they would never go." She was scanning the room all the while she unwrapped her bundle on the bar. Then she turned around to study me.

"Come," said Jacqueline to me. "This is Christine, who will take all your money if you let her. She is a saleswoman . . . Tiens! Christine, I have no time. A nightgown, that is all."

On the bar in the center of a broad expanse of wrapping paper and thick string, Christine spread an array of cotton-knit panties and nightgowns in bold solid colors.

Jacqueline picked out a rose-colored nightgown, threw it over her left shoulder, and walked to the cash register in the grocery store. The saleswoman followed, one eye on the doorway, alert to the sound of heavy boots.

"And the pants?"

"Those I have."

Jacqueline called from the cash register: "Sixty francs?"

"Sixty-five!" said the saleswoman.

A regular customer like me? "Sixty."

"Sixty-three. After that it's out of my own pocket."

Jacqueline returned with the money. The saleswoman put two pairs of panties on Jacqueline's right shoulder, one lavender, one bright blue. "Go ahead! Take them." She named a price, then made a pretense of walking away.

"No. I have plenty, I told you."

Christine took the pants from Jacqueline's shoulder, placed them in the middle of the bar and wrapped her parcel, carefully unknotting the twine and retying it.

"You'll take something," said Jacqueline, reaching for a bottle of wine. "It is weather for wolves!"

"It is my turn," said the saleswoman. "But, of course, you must drink," she added, turning to me. "I do not expect you to buy. This is my route. Good health."

We all drank.

As Christine opened the door to the street, her bundle under her arm, a workman entered, and she turned and winked at us before disappearing.

Madame Jacqueline wiped the bar and replaced the wine bottle beneath the mirror behind her.

"I look a sight," she said to her reflection. "And when, now, shall I go to Antony? . . . Oh, it is not an easy life for a poor, defenseless woman alone."

The actual hours per week at Jacqueline's Café did not add up to much. Nor could they be regarded as what anthropologists call "participant observation." Not really.

I learned to nurse along a glass of wine beyond normal expectations and remain an unintrusive part of life as it played out within the café. Once in a while it was inevitable that I get caught up in the celebration of a near-limitless number of felicitous events: birthdays, anniversaries (of marriage, years on the job, years lived in Vertier), a Baptism or First Communion or Confirmation of one's child (or the child of anyone in the café), any holiday, an unexpected windfall of good fortune, or a kind of generalized drink for better things to come. The café was tiny and rarely full, so that a shared "Salut!" all around was almost always feasible and affordable.

Jacqueline was onto me and empathetic, so long as I did not contribute to any diminution of activity. It was Jacqueline who contrived and circulated the story that a benign but vexing blood condition was at the root of my apparently stunted appreciation of wine. The fact that the wine was not a local product, and consequently could in no way be interpreted as a negative appraisal of the community resources, also bailed me out of censure. Nevertheless I made sure that I was not found wanting in terms of an occasional round.

But my participation in life at Jacqueline's was not comparable to that of the average resident who sought out the café for the real purposes it served in this small-knit community: a quick "on-the-thumb" swallow before the workman heads out on a cold morning to mix cement for a wall, the pleasant midday break that allows a busy housewife (with shopping bundles beside her) a congenial half hour before the endless chores of village housekeeping, a place to air good news and bad, a political arena or simply somewhere to voice one's reservations (widely shared) about the state of the world. In Vertier, the ups and downs of life were not always easily shared outside safehavens like Jacqueline's.

I sat and watched and was tolerated, but only tangentially involved . . . because I had limited credentials for membership.

These credentials would come but s-l-o-w-l-y as our little family settled in, and my presence was eventually validated by a shared need for the café's distractions.

Notes

[1] This chapter draws from Robert T. Anderson and Barbara Gallatin Anderson, *Bus Stop for Paris* (New York: Doubleday, 1965).

[2] "Grandmother" is used here as a term of respect.

2

The Anthropologist as Participant Observer
The Danish Cooking School

For real "participant observation" the cultural anthropologist must actively take on some portion of the script of
daily life within the community.

Participant observation is indispensable to fieldwork. We
seek it out. Often we venture out on some cultural tightrope,
never quite sure how high above the ground we really are.
Most of the time the fall—if it does come—is a modest one. Our
most vivid memories, however, are of episodes gone awry.
Accounts of these experiences are rarely seen as advancing
anthropological knowledge, and conventional wisdom has
weeded them out of most textbooks. And that's unfortunate.
Often it is when the anthropologist unwittingly breaches some

mundane social expectation, performing badly, that a community's priorities are made pointedly clear.

One venture into participant observation that comes to mind occurred in Denmark,[1] where I did my first fieldwork outside the United States on a small island in the Kattegat, the tumultuous sound that eventually links the Baltic and the North seas.

My plans to work in West Africa had fallen through. The research grant that took me to Denmark was that of my anthropologist husband, whom I assisted in documenting the transformation of a centuries-old maritime economy. A portion of the island had become a kind of bedroom extension of nearby Copenhagen, yet the "old village"—where we lived and where we had plunged five-year-old Katie into kindergarten—was remarkably intact. Architecturally and psychologically, Taarnby (not its real name) was still an extension of the sea around it.

Our thatched house lay close to the area where fishermen hung their nets to dry, pilot boats rocked within sight, and the land was often indistinguishable from the harbor's sifting gray fog.

The village was not without its charm. When the sun shone, and especially when some of the older women walked about in traditional dress, the effect was of a sudden time warp and entry into the world of Hans Christian Andersen.

My husband was fluent in Danish, and if any prerequisite to fieldwork was to burn itself into my brain, it was that of an adequate command of the field language before departure. I reached the field ill-prepared for work in Denmark, having had time to do little more than struggle through *You Can Say It in Danish*, a phrase book for tourists that armed me with such valuable phrases as "My glasses are broken" and "Give my regards to your aunt and uncle." In our initial weeks on the island I was to work these into local conversations with the greatest difficulty.

After two months of snail-like fieldwork I decided to find some low-keyed activity that would involve me casually, but more acceptably and challengingly, in village life. Something beyond the formal questionnaire interviews I had begun with the wives of pilots, fishermen and maritime crews. Participant observation.

My husband suggested that I should enroll in the cooking class offered for adults at the local high school on Monday and Thursday evenings from six to nine o'clock. It seemed a brilliant idea. I would learn what to do with all that strangely dissected meat I saw in butcher shops, and with those fish—great and small—that lay languidly shimmering, eyes staring, on enormous wood trays in the harbor. I would make the sweet soups everyone was so fond of: buttermilk, apricot, and beer soup with whipped cream and ground black bread. And I would ask why they had rid the island of vegetables and fruits.

Above all, I wanted to create a tray of those exquisite *smørrebrød* sandwiches, as complex as a medieval still life, perfectly crafted in line and color. And our home would become a Mecca for the pastry-obsessed housewives of the village, who could chat for hours about the appropriate icing for a cupcake.

The time was right. A new class was to begin the following week.

On Monday I changed my clothes three times before deciding on a camel-colored sweater and skirt. Over them I wore my venerable dyed-lamb coat, for my husband had warned me: "That place will be like an icebox."

Set among the thatched, peaked-roof cottages, the school building, with its poured-concrete architecture, looked as alien as a spaceship. I couldn't have been more nervous if I had been going to a ball at Fredensborg Castle. Clutching a small, folded apron, I found it was no easy matter to locate the front door, let alone the classroom. There seemed no break at all in the flat facade. I moved back into the middle of the cobbled street to get some perspective just in time for a man to maneuver his bicycle around me and dismount.

"Hello," he said, whisking the bicycle onto a rack.

"I don't suppose you'd know where the cooking school meets," I said. "The door is just to the side," he gestured. "I am going there, too." He moved rapidly ahead of me and then turned as I stood weighing his pronouncement. "Come! Come!" he urged. "The teacher is called Talia the Terrible. She will have our heads if we are late."

I followed him through a tunnel-like entrance to the far side of the building and into a classroom, bright with light and with white tiles that covered the floor and walls to a height of about eight feet. It looked rather like an empty swimming pool, except that almost at the point of entrance, and running crosswise, stood a great table with chair. And behind it a half dozen smaller tables for four were spaced to form a kind of restaurant. Along the far wall were several stoves. Sinks banked both sides of the room. On each side of the sinks were work surfaces, and above them cupboards had somehow been affixed to the tiles.

I shall never forget our teacher, Fru Rasmussen, alias Talia the Terrible. When she turned her full gaze upon me, I forgot every word of Danish I knew. Except that she was half again as tall and three times as wide, she reminded me of Helen Hayes as she looked in the late-show reruns of *A Farewell to Arms*, standing competently in the uniform and headdress of a World War I nurse.

Fru Rasmussen was laminated into an unsulliable, white buttoned-front dress that extended almost to her ankles and was of such stiffness that the elbow-length sleeves encircled, but did not touch, the skin of her generous arms. A triangle of the same taut cotton hid all but an inch of her iron-gray hair. Impassively, she lifted a large black cigar to her lips and waited for us to find seats.

"Abject apologies," said my guide, and I mumbled a repetition of his words. We slipped into two vacant chairs, so positioned that they afforded a profile view of Fru Rasmussen, who from that angle looked as if—perhaps without the cigar—she might be affixed to the prow of a sailing ship. Except for my cyclist friend, the class was female, and there were perhaps a dozen of us.

"Exactly twelve!" said Fru Rasmussen, who I was now convinced could read my thoughts. "And that is good," she continued. "Three tables of four. At every class we shall prepare a complete meal of four courses, with each person at a table responsible for one course. In this fashion each table prepares and consumes a full dinner. You will, therefore, not eat before you come. You will not smoke during the preparation, cooking, or consumption of food. Tobacco is permitted before or after class or during our ten-minute break."

We were then advised to choose our foursomes. With more tables than arithmetically feasible, given the four-to-a-table directive, we had a problem from the start. What ensued was an aberrant version of musical chairs as women anxiously circled the tables, weighing the consequences of where and with whom they might suddenly find themselves irrevocably seated. The first sorting produced two persons at five tables, with the bicycle rider and me left standing. Fru Rasmussen's left arm slashed the air with the precision of a symphony conductor.

"Be seated," she ordered. If she had in the same tone ordered me to leap to a tabletop, I should unhesitatingly have done so.

The bicycle rider and I quickly sat at an occupied table directly in front of us, thereby producing the first foursome—like some significant mutation in a precipitous evolutionary change. There followed a disorganized shuffling about as nervous partners rapidly occupied vacant chairs lest they be separated. At one point six women converged on an empty table that went to the swiftest and fittest. Eventually the remaining women faltered into place.

Her next directive was to "put on the smocks!" I knew this word only because a smock was a portion of the uniform required of schoolchildren.

My apron evoked a wan smile from Fru Rasmussen. "Charming," she said. And then, "On Thursday, a smock!"

We were shown where utensils, bowls, cutlery, and china were kept. We paid our fees and our names were entered into a ledger according to table membership, an undertaking that constituted a mass informal introduction. Socially we were roughing it. And I thanked God. True and proper Danish introductions require a complex etiquette that legitimizes the compulsive need of Danes to know everything about one another.

My cycling friend was Poul, an engineer. He was from the beginning entirely comfortable in a class of women. When Grete, whom I recognized as the assistant postmistress, ventured that he must be a gourmet, Poul said matter-of-factly, "Oh no! Not at all. It's simply that my wife is a dreadful cook."

Grete shook her head sympathetically.

"Oh, it's quite understandable," Poul continued. "You see she *hates* to cook. Always has, really."

He was buttoning himself into what looked like a white lab coat. It apparently passed inspection by Talia the Terrible, who accorded Poul one of her rare smiles.

So we were four. In addition to Grete, Poul, and I, there was Inge, who was blond and pretty and planning to be married as soon as she and her fiancé could find a place to live in Copenhagen, where he worked as apprentice to a silversmith. Inge was as assertive as Grete was timid. Poul was simply forthright. It seemed to me a fortuitous group, congenial and united. Together we should not be a total pushover for Talia the Terrible's juggernaut approach to Danish high cuisine.

We began with what I thought a humble enough assignment: cucumber salad, meat loaf, potatoes, and a sweetened berry compote, which is to Denmark what Jell-O is to the United States. Fortunately, or unfortunately as it turned out, the meat loaf was assigned to me—a decision that left the rest of the table faintly awed.

Food terms are a hellish but critical challenge in any language. If you can develop the faintest comfort with a culture's food vocabulary, with the words used for everyday fare, festive fare, spices, beverages, food for children, food for the sick, hot weather food, cold weather food, the never-to-eat foods (which in Denmark give you anything from hives to night blindness), you are halfway to bilingualism if you never learn another word. My *Danish Made Simple* listed thirty varieties of fish alone, only two of which I could identify with confidence, the eel and the stingray, and then only in their raw states. Why twenty-five vegetables and twenty fruits were listed I could not imagine, though I dutifully tried to commit them to memory. In two months I had seen or tasted only red cabbage, carrots, cucumbers, the ubiquitous potato (often prepared in two or three ways for a single meal), and lumpy apples, which got that way from being stored after harvest for months on attic floors and rotated lest they rot.

However, that first evening at cooking class I felt welling up within me an alien and buoyant sense of confidence. "I think this is going to be great," I told Poul.

Fru Rasmussen's kitchen was very orderly. Virtually everything was labeled. All the canisters. All the utensils. Even the great wire whisk had a sliver of paper affixed to its handle to assure that its identity was in no way to be a source of perplexity to the uninitiated. Henceforth it and other terms would be engraved on my mind, and in this easy fashion my vocabulary would soar in no time at all.

Each table was assigned its own inviolable work surface, ample and deep enough for four to work beside the stoves.

"In the preparation for dinner, it shall be my practice," said Fru Rasmussen, "to read aloud to the assembled class instructions for all courses." We were admonished to listen always "with all ears." After her oral instructions, she would hand a detailed recipe, typed on a card, to the appropriate chef.

"Each of you will be assigned a chef-and-table title. Thus, tonight Fru Anderson will be Meat Loaf Chef Two: 'Meat Loaf,' since at her table the responsibility for the main dish will fall on her. And 'Two,' since she occupies the table bearing the marker two." She nodded in my direction, reaffirming the assignment she had seen fit to allot me. Perhaps I was not on her hit list after all.

"Students will be addressed and will address one another by their chef-and-table titles," she continued in staccato tones. Use of Christian names or surnames (like the use of tobacco) was henceforth restricted to off-duty breaks.

Ingredients needed in the preparation of dinner were housed in open shelves above us; utensils were in open shelves below. There were curious miniature clipboards at fixed locations on the wall above each chef's work space, and to these appropriate recipes were to be attached. The location was high but readable for me. It was definitely at crouch level for Poul. In those first intense moments at our recipes, peering from odd positions, we must all have looked like a pack of hapless voyeurs.

There were two more ironclad rules: first, regardless of the oral presentation—made by Fru Rasmussen—one's own recipe was to be read from start to finish before one did anything in the kitchen; second, ingredients were to be gathered and used in the order of their listing unless instructions were given to the contrary.

The entire class was in action before I had finished the required reading of the recipe. It seemed a strange combination for meat loaf, but I knew the Danish predilection for sweets. If not swift, I was sure. I even drew a smile from Fru Rasmussen as she watched me scrape a knife across the top of a measuring cup. Thinking in grams and kilos normally gave me enormous difficulty, but tonight I was having no problems.

"You will all take a moment to observe Meat Loaf Chef Two," Fru Rasmussen commanded, "as she carefully but gently assures no more nor less than the required amount."

I felt very good and turned to beating two eggs (next item) authoritatively into the bowl. There followed an impressive sequence of spices whose names I could not translate and only two of which I could identify with certainty, salt and pepper.

Since the meat loaf would be the longest cooking, and since its chefs had been enjoined "to get on with it," I began to feel some pressure to keep pace with my colleagues, particularly when I heard oven doors opening and closing around me. I beat the ground veal and pork together with unrelenting strokes, though my arm was growing tired and heavy. Finally, having slid the pan into the small black and white oven, I joined the others and listened to the small talk about our coming feast.

Fru Rasmussen lit up another large black cigar. One woman smoked a smaller brown version that was in common use in the village. Poul lit his pipe. The wool skirt and sweater had been a mistake. I walked over and leaned against the tiles. Poul opened the back door and there was a rush of cool air, smelling of the sea. The women walked about, studying the cupboards and their contents.

Suddenly Fru Rasmussen lifted her left wrist, displaying her watch, and tapped the face of it with a fingernail. It had the clear finality of the timed seizure of an enemy encampment. "Meat Loaf Chefs will check their . . ." and there followed a word I could not understand. "The others will proceed to the setting of tables."

While Fru Rasmussen expounded on table settings and the intricacies of napkin folding (a Danish compulsion), I cautiously followed the Meat Loaf Chefs so that I might determine, undetected, the precise mission that had been assigned us. They touched nothing on or in the stove, but peered at what I immediately but belatedly recognized as timers fixed on the back panels. And at that precise moment I heard their joint ticking like the relentless activity of some agitated bomb.

I had not set my timer! I didn't even remember reading about a timer. Not that I would have recognized the word, but it must have been there somewhere, or maybe I had missed it in Fru Rasmussen's rapid verbal instructions. "How many minutes?" came Fru Rasmussen's voice.

"Twenty-seven! Twenty-five! Twenty-eight!" came the replies of the other Meat Loaf Chefs. There were a few heavy seconds of silence. And then I leaned with simulated interest over my stove, studying the back panel. "Thirty!" I called aloud. As it was, I had probably shaved four minutes off my actual baking time. Fru Rasmussen cocked her head to one side, giving full consideration to standard meat loaf deviations. For a moment I thought she was going to leave the group that was pulling dishes and flatware from the cupboards.

My heart was hammering. If she approached my stove, I intended either to slump to the floor, feigning heat prostration—a condition I was rapidly approaching anyway—or chance it and whirl the timer knob to thirty minutes. What disturbed me was that I had no idea how prominent a noise the latter course of action would create, but somehow it seemed a more dramatic move than the first.

Fortunately for everyone, she remained where she was and announced: "Napkin time! All chefs to the main table!"

For the next fifteen minutes we were occupied with making graceful white swans from starched white napkins—a feat I executed once but was never to duplicate. When at last the tables were properly set and inspected, the Salad Chefs had their moment. To them would routinely fall the additional responsibilities of "presenting" bread and butter and whatever condiments were appropriate to the meal. There were courteous *ohs* and *ahs* over the marinated cucumbers that had been scraped and sliced into delicate snowflake patterns.

Dinner was announced and we sat down. Fru Rasmussen sat at a separate table, the better to review and display samples from the efforts of each chef. A segmented dish, of the kind used at picnics, that keeps beans from running into salad, lay before her, except that hers was large indeed and had numerous sections. The four Salad Chefs had already deposited samples of their cucumbers for her review. Our individual servings lay in their cool delicacy in small dishes before each of us. Fru Rasmussen speared a single cucumber, and I could resist no longer. The cucumbers were lovely, if few, and I devoured them in several strokes of the fork. "Before beginning our salads," Fru Rasmussen started. I looked around our table. With their eyes mercifully lowered Poul and Grete and Inge were waiting. As was everyone else. I replaced my fork on my dish and the small sound reverberated from the tiles. "Before beginning our salads," Fru Rasmussen began again.

Poul looked distracted. "I smell something," he said quite audibly. Inge nodded. "Meat loaf."

"No," Poul said. Grete nodded her agreement. "It smells more like . . . caramelized potatoes."

"Before beginning our salads," Fru Rasmussen said again, enunciating now with clear displeasure. Her eyes were riveted on Poul.

"I know that smell," Poul persisted. "Browning sugar."

People were beginning to say that they smelled something. And then, before I could figure out why I found these pronouncements troubling, there was a great ping!

"Meat Loaf Chefs to the ovens," Fru Rasmussen called out, and I was on my feet, adrenaline coursing. Something in the back of my mind was surfacing, something with which my brain was struggling but was oddly reluctant to confront.

The stoves with their spindly iron legs and black and white enameled ovens suddenly looked as Danish and foreign as the schoolhouse flag. Apprehension lay on me like a damp towel. We were handed potholders. We opened the oven doors and, as directed, carried the pans, wreathed in steam, to our tables, where we placed them on tiles provided especially for them.

I walked, my pan wreathed not only in steam but in a powerfully emanating sweetness that soon penetrated the room like cheap perfume.

"It's rather dark for meat loaf, isn't it?" said Grete. It shone, glistening like a small, iridescent oil spill.

"However did you do that?" Poul asked, impressed. By now my meat loaf had attracted an audience. I went over to check the meat loaves at other tables. They were brown and much more plumped up. They did not shine. There was considerable milling about until Fru Rasmussen called for order. One had the feeling she was less in command of things. The white segmented sampling plate began circulating through the tables, picking up meat loaf samples as it went. Ours was the last.

"I'll do it," said Inge in the low, supportive voice one uses in the presence of the bereaved. She poised a dinner knife over the end of the meat loaf. The first gentle sawing produced nothing. She raised the knife, tip sharply downward, penetrating the meat at a right angle. The second thrust produced the kind of shattering one sees in vandalized unbreakable glass; the third, a portion of meat from which hung a kind of peanut-brittle jacket. Inge placed it on the plate, and the jacket fell back into place. I took the plate from her hands and carried it to Fru Rasmussen. A palpable silence had fallen over the room.

We agreed later that Fru Rasmussen displayed uncharacteristic gentleness. I believe she was in shock, but she was diplomatic when she spoke to me. "I am curious as to what innovations you brought to the recipe," she said, as nearly as I could translate.

If my Danish had been up to it, I would have told her that it was all I could do to keep up with the barrage of instructions, let alone embark on creative embroidery of them. Under the circumstances, my vocabulary shrank like some shaken thermometer to a new low, as it did under all situations of pressure. I did the only thing I could think of. I took Fru Rasmussen by the arm and steered her to the stove, above which still hung the fateful recipe. I stared at it as one might stare at the formula for a strychnine-laced cocktail. Within it, somehow, lay a dreadful secret.

With a precision born of muteness I pointed to the first ingredient and released my grip on her arm long enough to describe with thumbs and index fingers the arcs of two eggs. Then, resuming my grasp, I resolutely directed her eyes to the second listing, at which point I used both hands to lower the large canister of sugar. I placed it on the work counter and scrounged about until I found the four-gram measuring cup. I generated a forced smile to reenact her public praise of the precision with which I had expertly scraped my knife across the dry measure of sugar.

Then I hit an impasse. Meat. How to convey the proportions of veal and pork? Poul was at my side, and I found my voice. "What is it?" I asked.

There followed a very rapid exchange between Poul and Fru Rasmussen. Then Fru Rasmussen turned her full gaze upon me. But it was Poul who spoke:

"Say 'sugar.'"

"Mel," I said.

"Say 'flour.'"

"Melis."

"Close," Poul said. Then he turned, translating the exchange for Fru Rasmussen. A low moan escaped her lips as we both realized how, by confounding "sugar" with "flour," I had desecrated the meat loaf.

Eventually the class did get around to laughing, although not heartily. Since dinner at school had to serve as a real meal twice a week for the next six weeks, I loomed as a clear and constant menace. I had broken a cardinal rule of Danish culture: never stand between a Dane and his dinner. On that first evening, the generous dessert, expertly prepared by Poul, tempered but did not alleviate, concern about my presence.

At the next class I was made a Dessert Chef, a legitimate rotation except that I was charged with watching all the puddings cool on the chilly back stairs, ostensibly to insure their safety from animal predators. Actually it was a serious demotion. Another Dessert Chef assumed the cooking responsibility for our table.

At the third meeting I was restored to serve as Soup Chef Two. Chowder was on the menu, and like each of the Soup Chefs, I had the initial assignment of preparing the soup stock. Members of my table and other Soup Chefs gave me warm pats on the back and said encouraging things that only reinforced my feeling of being on probation. "We are with you all the way," Inge whispered as I slipped into my smock.

The first step in preparing the chowder was surgically removing the eyes from four large fish heads. Fru Rasmussen stood at my side ready to direct my hands through this routine procedure. She outlined with her finger the appropriate incision in the tissue of the head.

"He is very fresh," she said. "See how bright and clear the eye! If you do it properly, the eyes will simply pop into your hands."

The eye was bright and clear and fixed on me. I looked around the room at all the busy Soup Chefs. "Proceed," Fru Rasmussen said, taking firm hold of my fish. I picked up the knife and lowered the point of the blade to the fish head.

"Well?" said Fru Rasmussen.

I looked up and saw a woman open a bloody hand and drop something into a bucket. I heard "Pong! Ping!" as the objects hit bottom.

Then—as nearly as I remember—I took off my smock, solemnly shook hands with each of my tablemates (as good form requires), said good-bye to Fru Rasmussen, put on my lambskin coat, and walked out into the icy Danish night.

Poul and Grete and Inge forgave me and carried on as a threesome. At Christmas Poul invited our family to join his in a traditional goose dinner with all the trimmings—a meal he fixed himself.

My reputation as a high school cooking class dropout generated surprisingly favorable dividends. There was a consensus. No one as incompetent as I was could continue to be regarded as a serious threat to village life. The chief pilot's wife, who had eluded my attempts to arrange an interview with her, came to call, and in the course of her visit volunteered to teach me some of her family's favorite recipes. She was happy to do it, she insisted, "for the sake of the family."

I concluded that the village wives had drawn straws to stave off the starvation of my unfortunate husband and child, and that the chief pilot's wifc, Fru Strunge, had gotten the short straw.

Things were looking up.

Participant observation was the way to go!

Note

[1] This chapter is based on Robert T. Anderson and Barbara Gallatin Anderson, *The Vanishing Village: A Danish Maritime Community* (Seattle: University of Washington Press, 1964; and Barbara Gallatin Anderson, *First Fieldwork: The Misadventures of an Anthropologist* (Prospect Heights, IL: Waveland Press, 1990).

DYNAMICS
OF CULTURE

3

Cultural Identification and Cultural Confrontation

Indian Summer

The concept of culture, as anthropologists use it, is an elusive one. The first definition I committed to memory was that culture is learned, shared, and transmitted behavior. I still like it. The fact that it does not say everything that might be subsumed within culture's scope is evident from the debates that have raged over culture's parameters for more than a century.

In 1952, Alfred Kroeber and Clyde Kluckhohn, both renowned scholars and teachers, published a book called *Culture: A Critical Review of Concepts and Definitions*. Already definitions alone totalled 162. Today deliberation continues. And, I suppose, anthropologists should be seriously concerned only if debate stops.

Convictions as to the nature of culture range from the judgment that culture is basically self-evident to the less confident posture that culture is symbolic and undecipherable. In other words, you can look at culture in terms of a people's coping mechanisms which, over time, have taken on a profile as distinctive as a thumbprint; or, you can concede, as some have, that no culture can really be understood by an outsider and be guided by less ambitious goals.

In this, as in many other anthropological issues, fieldwork is to theory as air is to fire, illuminating the enticing scope of culture's complexity... at least it was for me, in the context of a summer of work in India.[1] There, like it or not, I learned a great deal about culture's complexity in the context of cultural identification and cultural confrontation.

It all began when a national foundation circulated the announcement of its intention to bring together in India a small group of American professors whose coursework included units on India, but who had never set foot in the country. I sent off for the application packet. I might well be eligible.

My social organization course routinely included discussion of India's *jajmani*, or mini-caste system. Also, assigned reading on trends and dilemmas within India's health care system was part of my seminar in medical anthropology.

The grant promised "a summer exploring the immense cultural diversity of the subcontinent of India and one of the world's largest populations." The foundation also let it be known that some demands would be made on the chosen candidates' expertise—a few lectures and some meetings with local groups. These obligations, we were assured, would make modest demands upon our time. I applied.

Over the six months before notification as to outcome, my optimism waned. Belatedly it occurred to me that I should have had my application looked at by a colleague who had married an Indian woman and who spent much time in village India as well as in New Delhi, where the orientation sessions would take place for those fifteen fortunate scholars chosen for "Summer-in-India."

I asked him to lunch, after which—forewarned—he scanned my proposal. When he had finished, he folded the dozen or so pages and put them back in the envelope.

"Well . . .?" I asked.

"Why didn't you come to me before you sent this off?" He gave a great sigh and turned to me with baleful eyes.

"Bad as that."

"God, no." He gave a little laugh. "The problem is you're liable to get the damn thing . . . *Summer* in *India*."

To my surprise I did. And later . . . much later, during the three months and 10,500 miles of moving about in India (someone kept track), his words would float unbidden across my mind.

India was a great experience. No doubt about that. I include here some reflection on it because India spoke to the phenomenon of culture with a kind of distilled "fast-forward" intensity unmatched in my experience. I learned about the tenacity of cultural identification, the challenge of new formulas for living, and the in-between world of cultural realities within which cultural anthropologists routinely live out their fieldwork and much of their lives.

I arrived in New Delhi on a much delayed flight at 2:30 A.M. The temperature was 103 degrees Fahrenheit. The next morning, in the comfortable "board room" of an Indian government office, members of our group met one another and the sari-clad representative of the Indian government who capably would see us through an intensive three-day orientation period. Our group consisted of five professors of history, three of philosophy, two of theology, one of sociology, one of English, one of mass communications, one of political science—and one of anthropology. We were thirteen men and two women.

The fourth day in Delhi was to become a part of the "memorable-moments" folklore that rapidly took shape within the group. Before leaving the United States, we had all had the required immunization and booster shots. We carried the papers to prove it, as well as documentation of successfully passed physical examinations. It remained that we should be instructed in health precautions to be taken within India.

That made sense. Our "health maintenance" instructor, Miss Dorsey, was a former British army nurse and uncompromisingly serious about her assignment. After about ten minutes watching her, most of us had the same reaction. With a common vision we mentally put her back in military uniform. Her voice was a monotone of tragic prediction. Clearly, it was dicey if any of us would make it through the months ahead permanently unhandicapped. She described a litany of impending conditions that would have sent the less valorous racing for the airport.

She meant well. But she made it clear that few of us looked endowed with the marginal wisdom critical to self-care in a disease-plagued universe. To compensate, she had a resolution at hand: equipment and medication each of us reasonably could not be without.

Some of it was logical. But half of us would have expired of heat prostration (given the temperature) dragging all the stuff about: kepi hats, canteens, snakebite kits, a large black umbrella, together with a voucher for stout knee-high boots within which—we soon learned—a layer of fuzzy white mold formed if they were closeted for more than eight hours and into which sweaty feet released pools of water.

Our time was almost equally distributed between rural and urban areas of India. While a portion of the program was structured with scheduled visits and visitors, we were for the most part free at each stop to go where we chose and speak with whomever we wished. In a country of eighteen language groups, a fundamental problem was anticipated, and our guides and translators changed with the region or the circumstance.

Together or as individuals, we talked with families, farmers, factory workers, politicians, hospital patients and health workers, schoolchildren, fishermen, sidewalk dwellers, mill owners, monks, college students, Peace Corps volunteers, village leaders and many others. We traveled by bus, vans, plane, local taxis, bicycles, jeep, and once by elephant.

The sights and sounds and smells of India poured in and out like unpredictable tides. Our bodies, minds, and emotions seemed always being put to some kind of test, intensely engaged.

India was gorgeous and ugly. In Ahmedabad seemingly limitless wealth was almost casually displayed at a mill owners' luncheon for us. We were twenty-five at a single table, whose length I have never seen replicated. Behind us were twenty-five servants. One stood at each chair, anticipating any conceivable need, making us all hugely conscious of every gesture. Walls and cabinets were dotted with museum-quality treasures. On the lawn peacocks made puzzling sounds that I initially credited to some kind of dove. Five of our hosts—there were no women—wore Western business suits; their cuff links were of gold and/or precious gems. Gracious, informed, and thoroughly comfortable in English, the mill owners helped us understand the region, the changing social systems, the selective proliferation of Western technology and communication, the schools and health facilities being constructed—under their direction—to attract workers and to replace, at a tempered pace, the former village control of craft specialists.

Calcutta was a different script. A half-million people lived on the sidewalks. Some had fled as whole families from social upheavals and fighting in the north. For two days I joined part of Mother Teresa's team, and with two Catholic nuns (one a German M.D. and the other an Italian nurse) patrolled the city in a makeshift ambulance. (This was before the present pope gifted them with a fine new one.) Mainly we picked up the dead and dying, and fetuses from garbage cans. The dying were brought back to a two-tiered "hospital" of stringed cots where they were sponge-bathed, their nails trimmed, and despite food and limited medication, almost predictably died of preexisting conditions and—like the fetal remains—were humanely disposed of.

Not every community offered such extremes of high drama, and the weeks piled up as we made our way through the transverse mountain ranges running east to west across the Indian triangle and into the central plateaus, as well as the startlingly tropical tip of India, where in the midafternoon young boys would shinny up trees before any of us even *felt* the heavy first drops of what had become a daily afternoon avalanche of raindrops—which our hypochondriac insisted hurt.

Villages of two hundred to two thousand and a roster of neighborhoods in towns and cities put up with us and more often than not made us welcome. We were tourists too. We saw and would recall with joy the Taj Mahal, the pink city of Jaipur, the lush palaces of Udaipur—and wonderful Dal Lake in Kashmir, where I lived briefly on a houseboat.

But the most memorable *markers* of our days in India indisputably lay in the ever-changing spectrum of bath and toilet facilities, available or unavailable to us, as the miles piled up and our bodies reacted.

Only one member of the team failed to complete the program. And that had nothing to do with the intermittent bouts of gastric or intestinal problems that none of us wholly escaped. Against *all* counseling, one of our historians, whose justifiable concern about rodents had grown to obsession, persisted in checking nightly with a flashlight under his bed or cot for rats. On this particular night he drew the bunk closest to the kitchen and offended a rat who took the offensive, sending his attacker into a spectacular leap. When he regained the stone floor, it was with two badly sprained ankles, and we shipped him home.

In fairness it must be said that none of us escaped *culture shock*. But some people wore surprisingly well, and little by little I became impressed with the adaptive mechanisms that seemed variously at work. I am referring to processes that served in part to neutralize the effect of shock and to allow some help in functioning until we had passed the "crisis" phase and were capable of working within the host culture.

Culture shock designates the massive psychic reaction that takes place within individuals plunged into a culture vastly different from their own. The "shock" imagery suggests some resultant failure in appropriate response mechanisms, a derangement of control related to psychic injury or incapacitation. Basically it has to do with the forced accommodation of social elements that are normally part of an alien tradition and hence not "normal" for us. We are caught up in patterns of living, and standards of judgment, vastly different from those with which we are familiar and in whose logic we find security and identity.

Cultural anthropologists, despite their training, have no immunity from culture shock.

Culture shock is a phenomenon associated generally with a culture-change cycle that terminates, not with successful rooting in the new culture, but with a final retransplantation back to the mother culture. And in ways that became apparent to me in India, that home culture never let go of us, although its continuing hold was often repressed, displaced, and hence obscured.

It was the dynamics of that repression that began for the first time to absorb my attention in India. For I suggest that we survived, each of that team in India—with the one unfortunate exception—because we were able in shock (or perhaps *because* of shock) to draft an interim framework of cultural support, neither Indian nor the familiar, dominant American one we knew and lived on a daily basis. What we created was a hybrid prop that combined whatever old cues from our native culture could be recruited to immediate field usefulness and whatever supportive elements of the new culture (Indian) that could in some way be conventionalized.

Let me illustrate. The first clue I had in the field of the dynamics of this process was the regularity with which I was having a kind of dream different from my usual dreaming patterns. Also, on awakening there seemed to trail into consciousness a déjà vu quality. When I tried to identify what distinguished my "Indian" dreaming, I recalled this same unusual dream quality when I had been last in the field. I did not, as I had then, dismiss my interest. Instead I encouraged other members of the Indian team to speak about their current dreams. The pattern took more concrete shape, for little by little it became clear that many of us—most of us—were dreaming essentially within a definitive and a shared framework of personages and settings. In another four weeks (well over a month after our arrival) the character of dreaming changed for most of us. And though the group differed in individual timetables, a third and final shift in dream patterning occurred for all before the summer in India was over. I shall describe these sequences and suggest their relatedness to adaptation to culture shock.

In the first phase of our dreaming, during our first nights in India, few of us dreamed of spouses or children or of colleagues and friends. Our dreams were peopled heavily with figures involved not in our present, but in our past lives: old school chums, people from neighborhoods in which we had once lived, young men and women we had gone out with but not thought of for years. Insofar as people out of our current lives were involved in our dreams, they were largely tangential to the active social world of which we were a part when we left the United States; our homes or offices or campuses were not prominent. One man dreamed of a vacation spot, another of a distant neighborhood in his home city. Often the characters from the past brought their own settings along: a former classroom, a car we had once owned. When the setting was foreign, it did not look like the India we were in. Sometimes it was glossily exotic. We rarely dreamed of one another.

After more than a month in India and much movement, there was a change reported in the dream patterning. Families were entering the context of dreams, but almost shyly. One man reported dreaming for the first time since he had left the United States of his wife, "but she simply talked to me from the doorway." Another dreamed he was having lunch with a colleague, but the table was broad and they could not converse easily. A third watched his children fly kites from a considerable distance. Some dreamed of new Indian acquaintances, but often they were doing peculiarly un-Indian things: playing cards, riding in a sports car, or sitting in a conventional, though unfamiliar, Western house. One professor woke remembering that in his dream he touched his hand to his head and felt the folds of an Indian turban. In one, our Indian woman guide was smoking and spoke English without any accent at all, though actually she did not smoke, and her speech was difficult to follow with the rolling Kerala accent.

In the final phase of dreaming, Americans were Americans and Indians were Indians, and the dream world resumed its old order except that the spectrum of personages and settings had widened. The professor whose wife had stood in the doorway reported that in dreams she had come to him. One of the women recalled the quality of her children's laughter as she heard it in her dreams. There were more distinctly Indian dreams, and these were more representative of Indian life as it was. In these Indian dreams we participated as Americans, and there was no more mixed identification, as in the turbaned-professor dream. Some dreamed of Indian settings in which spouses, siblings, and children mingled as a matter of course with Indians.

My interest in dreams began as more a diversion than a serious concern. I documented them in a daily journal along with data about current interviews and field appointments. However, in about the third week of our fieldwork my attention was drawn to a new development. An Indian farmer asked me the English word for a fruit (which appeared on a poster). What came instantly to mind was not the English but the French word for it, and I said it aloud before I could stop myself. It was a few seconds before I came up with "grapefruit," and then by the indirect mechanism of translation from the French. Later, when thinking about the incident, I recalled a similar situation when in the early weeks of fieldwork in my French village, I found it simpler sometimes to translate, in speech, from English to Danish than from English to French—though I was far less conversant in Danish.

Of the same order, it seemed to me, as my trouble with "grapefruit" was our philosopher's sudden, embarrassing reference to his present wife of ten years by his first wife's name. Our sociologist could not remember at what resort the family had vacationed the previous summer, but in a rush of memory recalled to mind the telephone numbers of houses he had lived in over a fifteen-year period. Our professor of English spent a morning harassing us for the title of a song that had entered his head and whose melody he couldn't rid himself of and which turned out to be a World War II ballad. One of our historians became preoccupied with direction, in a way that recalled for me the acute consciousness of the Balinese of their position in relation to surrounding space and their fear of disorientation or "paling." He was constantly asking guides "Which way is north?" so that he could not, for example, participate in the tour of a village or temple without first establishing his position in relation to the India around him.

Traditionally, of course, the content both of dreams and of memory and speech lapses have provided rich insights into the distinctive logic of the psychological and cultural systems that direct human activity. Certainly the psychic props of repression and displacement and identification were there in the Indian dreaming. I suggest, however, that what I was also recording in dribs and drabs was the masked operation of a continuing cultural system to whose logic and support each of us remained bound, and to which we turned for psychological recharging and for cultural refuge.

Sleep suspends the principal function of waking life, reacting to reality by perception and action. During sleep the frame of reference may shift. We find refuge from the demands that are important in coping with reality. At the same time, however, in the waking state, as the memory and speech lapses suggest, thinking and feeling are not entirely subject to the limitations of the present time, and space of the present cultural order.

Let me state it as simply as I can. I think that our culture was continuing to communicate with all fifteen of us and that this communication was necessary for our psychic health and our social survival. When we left the United States, we had not ruptured, but merely suspended, the personal and social links that had from a preverbal period of our respective existences formed the basis for our "translation" or internalization of experience. In India, culture shock set in when we had to adapt to a drastically new input system on a personal and social level—new demands, new food, new language, new weather, new transportation, new philosophy, new harassments, and new pleasures, too; not all bad, not all good, but different. The addition of the new does not mean that the old was subtracted, that the old tried-and-true cultural basis for activity vanished. It was dormant largely because in its dominant forms it was inappropriate to most challenges: there was no American food; English language was of little help in most of rural India, where cars were virtually nonexistent. In addition, the United States was too dreadfully and painfully absent in its familiar cultural context. Our spouses and children were not going to be around for a while, and the fiction that they were was not one that we could easily conjure. In other important ways, too, the dominant links to our culture had been denied us. Consequently, we sought refuge in more plausible though less dominant cues of our continuing identity. *We created a secondary system of cultural identification.* We fell back on a substitutive but plausible order of reality.

This meant that often we had to go back in time or draw upon very peripheral links to unearth a personal and cultural image unchallenged by the field circumstances we faced in India. It did not matter that it was sometimes a dated or tangential image. What mattered was that this secondary system of cultural identification served temporarily as the anchor we needed during this critical period when we seemed to float out of reach of the old yet unanchored in a new environment. We could and did produce images of persons and situations (out of our own or a fantasized culture) with which we could relate comfortably. Through our dreams we were free of India, as we wanted to be after a day of coping. We recharged. And these dreams chronicled with surprising faithfulness the tremulous course along which we moved to the amelioration of shock and to adaptation in the field situation. In the first phase we cushioned ourselves almost completely from the painful present in which we could function neither as Americans nor as Indians. In dreams we were in full cultural retreat. In the second, we admitted small shock waves and then only if properly dissipated, still evading too Indian or too American stimuli. Eventually we could think "Indian," and then the character of our dreams and memories reflected it. We could and did admit Indian content and character.

Awake but on a subconscious level, we dredged up when needed the bulwark of old songs, familiar people, safe places. On other levels, too, the old cultural props were supportive. Distressed at first by some Indian odors, we recalled new-mown hay, the smell of bay rum, baked pies—from our youth. We hungered for American foods, many of which we had rarely or never eaten.

Some writers have referred, usually lightly, to the culture shock involved in returning to the United States, particularly after an extended field trip of, say, two years. But I don't think this is quite the same thing. It involves adaptation, yes. Often we are unprepared for the unfamiliarity of what we anticipated would be comfortingly familiar. And sometimes the field culture takes on a retrospective appeal beyond that which it actually afforded. But this returning is an experience of a different order. Actually, it is a kind of cultural reentry. In this situation, we are *not* without cues, the language, the semantic with-it-ness whose absence totally submerged us in the field. And I think, too, it is different because, as the Indian experience suggests, we have reordered but never abandoned our connection with that culture.

A telling development in these adaptive phenomena occurred late in the summer, it seems to me. Some team members had problems resuming fully their old identity when it came time to do so. There was a point for many where, when they could at last anticipate that plane ride home, there developed a startling nostalgia for "their" India. Some expressed concern about "getting back into the rat race." I think too it explains the often documented "unusual" behavior of tourists who find themselves caught up in adventures, sometimes romantic ones, that seem even to themselves out of character.

These are products, I suggest, of the identity crisis that accompanies the mixed cultural affiliation that is a part of these processes of adaptation to culture shock.

I am going to leave it there because the data frankly do not warrant greater mileage. They do suggest, however, that a counteractive phenomenon as powerful as culture shock is influential in the field situation. Just as the new culture reaches out and involves us, like it or not, so the old reaches out, but with a clinging hand. It helps assure not only our adaptation to the new culture, but the continuity of the old. It does this by shaping a protective secondary system of cultural identification that cushions us psychically through the more threatening phases of culture shock. And through it all, to facilitate our eventual return, the old culture waits, like a challenged beauty with a young competitor, working her old lures, knowing that when all is said and done and we have had our little adventure, we will return to her—as we both have known all along that we would.

Note

[1] A much similar version of this chapter appeared in *American Anthropologist*, 73, 5, (October, 1971).

4

Cultural Survival
On the Trail in Thailand

Most anthropologists have the good sense to target one geographic area (often sizable) for the bulk of their fieldwork, returning with whatever regularity schedules permit to the Far East or Europe or an American locality—building reservoirs of data and familiarity.

Gradually a flow of publications (vital to research and funding) documents the anthropologist's progress and sophistication about the chosen area and its people. In international and regional conferences, healthy dispute flourishes about research findings and their theoretical implications. Professional journals thrive on reporting them.

This "connectedness" of anthropologists spurs the need for further work. It serves as a safeguard against tunnel vision. The comparative and historical approach of ethnology derives from it. Thus, the nuances of Japanese social organization take on keener meaning when compared with alternative models. Samoan child-rearing patterns, however laudatory, profit from a look at different scenarios of enculturation in places where daily life routinely makes harsher demands on families. Similarly, Tibetan resolutions of high-altitude living are brought into richer focus by time spent in the Andean highlands. The Russian peasant is like, yet in surprising ways unlike the French peasant so that we explore why and how and toward what benefit these differences develop. Sometimes the published findings of other anthropologists provide the insights we want. At other times we go out and look for them ourselves.

In seeking answers, cultural anthropologists work most effectively in the context of one or more topical specializations: kinship, for example, or political organization, religion, art, culture change, medical anthropology. The list is long. These, like geographic concentrations, may develop out of graduate training or personal interest . . . or chance. An extraordinary amount of cultural anthropology derives from just plain serendipity, the apparent aptitude for making fortunate discoveries—the irresistible opportunity or, simply, a challenge.

Much of the work is carried out in a relatively unstructured, wide-ranging, exploratory fashion. Although a narrow, controlled focus is recognized for some dimensions of study, ethnological research methodology stems, not from the laboratory nor from statistical correlations, but from a natural history type of commitment to field investigation, where the essential mandate is to go out and find out what is there . . . admittedly an approach that can reap unanticipated consequences. My unscheduled sortie into the mountains of north Thailand comes to mind.

I was on my way to Moscow for an assignment in what was then the Union of Soviet Socialist Republics. At the last minute I scheduled a week's stopover in Thailand, a country I had long wanted to know more about. Bangkok, with its congestion and tourist-deluged attractions, soon proved uninviting. So, somewhat impetuously, I flew north to Chiang Mai, both a city and the name of Thailand's largest province—encompassing over 22,000 square miles, much of it home to long-resident hill tribes. A colleague had spoken lovingly of the place and given me the name of a tribal center directed by a British team.

On the plane I found myself seated next to Bill Blair (not his real name), an Australian I had met two days before at Timland, a kind of Thai Disneyland with mini-demonstrations of everything from Thai boxing to classic dancing and cock fights. The two-hour trip in a small DC-3 had none of the pomp of the Thai International flight out of Hong Kong during which meals were served on China plates in a series of courses, and dinner was followed by an excellent French brandy on a tray adorned with fresh flowers. In the skies over Chiang Mai we were offered cream puffs (which neither of us ate), biscuits, an excellent banana, a very dry orange, and tea. As we landed, I found myself wishing I had pressed my U.S. colleague further about the region we were entering. I did have the name of a hotel.

Chiang Mai looked great, a relatively compact, manageable town—mountains piled up in the distance. I got around the first morning by hiring a pedaled trishaw (called *samlor*). Once I'd gotten a sense of the place I walked everywhere. It was late November. The weather was cool.

My hotel looked like a dirigible hangar from the outside. The interior was grander, with plush red carpet and lots of white marble in the lobby. To my surprise the sizable dining room was virtually empty. Food and service were first-rate but with a visible oversupply of waiters standing about.

The afternoon brought disappointment.

At the tribal center, the British-born husband and wife team looked at my passport, asked a few questions, and told me it would be impossible to go up "into the hills" because no guide would be available before my scheduled departure. Going alone was quite out of the question . . . on that they were firm. What did I want to do there anyway? Well, I had read somewhere about a split-bamboo irrigation system used with success in the area and that intrigued me, but mainly I just wanted to prowl around. See what was there. They continued to shake their heads. Perhaps the next time . . . if I would let them know in advance of my visit.

I left the center and roamed rather disconsolately about. What was so complicated about finding someone who knew the hills? They must have the names of a dozen qualified guides. When I returned to the hotel, I must have conveyed something of my mood to Jai, the manager, who was at the desk. In no time at all (in retrospect, too swiftly) I was caught up in arrangements for me to leave the next morning for an overnight in Chiang Mai's hills. And, after a couple of animated phone calls (in Thai) during which Jai twice thumped the desk and alternately frowned and smiled into phone, he told me the cost (fairly steep, I thought) and outlined the general route.

"Do not worry," he said. "Everything is arranged. Everything will be one-hundred-percent lovely."

I was not the least worried. In any case, not then.

The dining room looked no more appealing than it had at lunch, so I went into the bar where—a notice in my room advised—"many little hot things" could be ordered "at every hour." And there at a small table sat my peripatetic Australian friend, Bill Blair. The hotel he had booked had proved a disaster and he remembered my mentioning this one. He was apologetic.

"No problem," I said. I found myself pleased to have someone to talk with. The table was full of "little hot things."

Blair, it seems, worked with a company that produced film and related products on an international scale for everything from instant cameras to industrial consumption. Beyond that I understood little except that access to good clean water—and lots of it—was pretty important somewhere along the production process. He wanted to look around locally . . . but *briefly*. His wife was seven months pregnant with their first child, and he was eager to get back to her.

"In any case," he went on, "'ol Jai' . . . at the desk just promised to fix me up with a guide and I leave in the morning for an overnight in the hills."

And that's how the two of us wound up headed for a village of the Hmong (called Meo by the Thai), the country's second largest tribal group.

"Swidden" cultivators, the Hmong seek out a forest site, cut and burn the trees and foliage. The ashes are allowed to cool and then seeds and shoots are planted, to be watered by rains and irrigation networks. This "slash-and-burn" cultivation is destructive of land. It depletes soil, so that farmers and families must eventually move on to slash and burn yet another virgin site. For subsistence, the Hmong grow rice and maize. For profit and the continuing insurance of their cultural independence they grow opium.

But of all this Blair and I were then wholly unaware. And if what follows is to make any sense at all, I need to share with the reader some relevant data about which we were equally uninformed as we set out on our "little adventure"—Jai's analogy.

As of last count (1998) Chiang Mai had some forty registered trekking agencies serving the surrounding hill area. The first were established twenty years before, which means that when we took off, few outsiders were wandering around the notorious Golden Triangle area north of the Kok River.

The year was 1967—after the full-scale military intervention of the United States in Vietnam in 1965. And *before* the signing of the Paris Agreement that brought withdrawal of American military forces at the end of 1972. The Golden Triangle is an area of some 75,000 square miles wrapped around the borders of Burma, Laos, and Thailand, and the major source of home-grown opium in the world, most of which was then being exported through north Thailand. Some opium was refined into heroin, principally in Burma's jungle laboratories.

The Vietnam War had itself proved an unanticipated boost in the popularity and availability of drugs. Commendable humanitarian efforts had reputedly expanded to include the ongoing purchase and transportation of drugs among our allies.[1]

Of all this, Blair and I were oblivious. Nor were we dwelling upon such facts as: opium is easily portable and grows best in high mountains (through which we would be climbing), is generally harvested between late November and February, and is a permanent attraction to banditry. Nor could we have known that Chang Chi Fu ("Prince of Prosperity"), better known as Khun Sa, a half-Shan, half-Chinese warlord and regarded as one of the world's most prolific drug dealers, was (with his private army) further tightening his control from headquarters reputedly north of Chiang Mai near Mae Salone. No friend of the United States, Khun Sa would later offer payment for the murder of Americans (whose government is said to have put a price on his head: only a humiliating and enraging $25,000). Dozens of U.S. citizens would leave Thailand.

The next morning, having breakfasted on poached eggs, toast, and hot tea, Blair and I found our guide waiting beside Jai in the lobby. After a polite round of introductions, and my stumbling through a phonetically pathetic version of a Thai greeting, we left the hotel under the protective care of Keena, a ninety-pound woman who might have been all of seventeen.

The driver of the car was far from fragile. Somewhere between burly and fat, he kept his eyes straight ahead, except for an expressionless nod as we two slid into the back and Keena took the seat beside him. Little had been said about our precise itinerary beyond the hotel manager's assurance that we would have a lovely time, a lovely trip. "Lovely" was Jai's favorite, all-purpose English adjective. I was confident he'd be ready with it if we were being carted off to execution.

Driving is on the left in Thailand, and Thais drive inches apart with frightening confidence. Our driver was no exception. Not until the vegetation began to thicken and I could feel the car climbing did my body begin to unwind. I hadn't had much sleep the night before. The room's air-conditioner was given to erratic rattles of vagrant parts, and it wasn't until I felt a nudge in my side that I realized I'd dozed off. Blair had wakened me. The road under us had turned to packed earth, and we bumped along, lifting red-brown sprays of dust as we went. Then, precipitously, we stopped. There was nothing more than sky around us. Sky everywhere. We could have been in the cockpit of a plane.

The driver got out of the car, unfolding into the tallest, broadest Thai I'd ever seen. He came around to the rear (there was *nothing* in front of us) and stood there until Keena joined him. Whatever the discussion was about, they were in disagreement. The road had narrowed to the edge of a rocky trail pointing downhill like a waterslide, which it must have resembled in monsoon conditions. Scattered shrubs clung to blackened earth at the trail's edges. Slash-and-burn country. Beyond were thicknesses of trees in staggered clumps and a panorama of undulating hills.

We got out of the car to face a smiling, nodding Keena. She pointed ahead. Apparently there was consensus: it was "do-able." We started downhill. After about fifty feet I looked back. The car was still there like some postmodern art form on a pedestal. Keena turned too and waved, and the car backed away. We were on our own.

I followed Keena. Bill brought up the rear. Our guide was surefooted and quick; she knew exactly where she was going—a village of some two hundred Hmong more than a mile distant. Blair was big for the trail and twice slipped and fell. The second time he got up rubbing his knee, his teeth clenched in pain.

"We're close now," Keena offered.

I heard a little bell. A man came into view walking beside a pony on a small rise where our trail crossed another. Two fat saddles added to the animal's middle and caught my eye immediately. Of some kind of straw or fiber, they were woven as studiously as petit point. A larger twosome would never have cleared the trail; man and horse were distinctive and handsome. As I stared, a pale spray of four or five orchids lifted and fell behind the man's head, like some elegant photo out of *National Geographic*. In my pocket was a small camera, loaded with film enough for thirty slides. My imagination was already projecting a gratifying lecture or two for my classes on the world of the highland Hmong. But somehow the use of a camera seemed not indicated. Keena moved to where the man stood, eight or ten feet from us. They spoke. He looked at us and, when the brief exchange was over, smiled and moved unceremoniously on with his slim animal and its bulging cargo.

Hmong villages blend so well with the surrounding countryside that it was a surprise to find ourselves in the midst of one.

This harmony of house and hills is something the Hmong purposefully seek. Symmetry is enhanced by their reluctance to construct new houses directly in front of or behind an existing one, and thus run the risk of confusing visiting ancestral spirits who prefer to travel in straight lines. Ancestors are needed upon a death in the family, for counseling, or simply invited.

House peaks seemed to slope to ground level and were thickly thatched. At closer range we could see the stubby walls of bamboo and roughly hewn wood, constructed with little apparent concern about gaps between the panels. But these, I would learn, are intentional and functional, letting smoke out and air in, just as the extended roofs carry off rain. There were no chimneys.

Some dwellings were impressive in size. Part of the illusion of length was the apparent absence of *doors*. How did people get in and out? I got this dilemma across to Keena with the aid of pantomime.

She was tolerant of my communication style but apparently had decided it was time to move on to a more articulate phase as guide. Her English took a dramatic surge for the better.

"Doors are at the rear of the house—avoiding mud slides and descending tigers."

The sun had passed overhead into a Western sky. Everything looked deserted. We moved about thirty feet downhill where the terrain had been purposefully leveled and there in the "front" of the house were several children, a woman of indeterminate age, and an old man sitting on a mat smoking a long pipe. The boys were playing with tops. All heads lifted at the sight of us.

The woman's clothes had an elegance the house did not. The immediate effect was more of a costume than a dress. Her soft-jacketed top and ankle-length skirt were of marine-blue cloth, fluid and graceful. As she approached, embroidery and appliqué work became evident on designs defining the open collar and sleeve edge. A necklace of wide silver lay around her throat—striking in its rich simplicity. A mass of black hair had been pulled almost to the top of her head in a rounded bun (made, I would learn, of previously trimmed hair). Loose gray-black strands lay around her face, and now she pushed them away as she studied us and gave a nod of recognition.

Her eyes fixed on Bill Blair. Her chin went up. The whole posture was of . . . rebuke . . . or challenge. Nothing easy to read but the flip side of warm and friendly. I would have settled for tolerant. Somehow I was okay; Bill Blair was not.

But Keena preempted whatever might otherwise have followed. Smiling benignly, she spoke to the woman, her voice all stroking tones. I had no idea what she said, but the woman was now beaming at us. We moved on. A hundred feet from the clearing, was one of the larger houses, its peaked roof impressive. It was where we would stay.

"What was all that back there?" Blair asked, disturbed, as I was, about our reception and the sudden dissipation of obvious displeasure about something.

"That was the headman's wife," Keena said. "Word was sent to her that I was bringing a woman to the village. No man was expected. The hill people have grown very, very unhappy about strangers coming." The ready smile returned. "But there is no need for worry. I have told her you are married."

"Married!" It was a joint cry. Blair and I froze in our tracks.

But Keena was unruffled. "Think of it as a marriage of convenience. There was no other way. It was only this morning I myself learned that you are not husband and wife. By then the car had come and the driver. It was all arranged."

Two things were now eminently clear. The all-knowledgeable Jai had collapsed two potentially intrusive presences (an anthropologist and a single male) into one cozy, uncomplicated, married tourist duo—absorbed with nothing but themselves. But what neither Bill Blair nor I could understand was *why* the rampant xenophobia?

"What's the harm in a single male, for heaven's sake?" I asked.

"It is their way," Keena said, which of course was no answer at all.

One thing for sure. After our death-defying ride from Chiang Mai and our acrobatic trek into Hmong country I had no intention of reliving it in reverse without so much as a decent look around.

A dog ventured out from a shallow recess under the house and approached us only to bark wildly and dash off. On one side was a fenced garden planted with herbs and some kind of chile. On the other, an elevated coop. Hens were audible.

"Where is everybody?"

"In the fields."

"Everybody?"

"Just about . . . harvest time." She was poking around the soil near the foundation. "They've left us a key."

"A key?"

"There are many valuables and much traffic."

Traffic? We'd run across one cow, a few goats, and a sizable pig. The key was gigantic. The lock made an audible screech as she turned it and we stepped in for the first look at where we'd stay.

The floor was earthen. Light came from the vertical gaps in the windowless wall construction. Gradually the house took on shape. The immediate effect was that of some minimalist stage set, complete with two elevated platforms, one higher and more complex than the other. What internal walls did exist were recessed along the main elevated platform, like giant mail slots but ceilingless.

"Sleeping compartments," Keena explained.

"What do they do about doors? . . . I mean . . . everything's open."

"Not needed. It is very dark at night. Besides, downstairs there are fires."

Sure enough, directly before us was a good-sized hearth, though at the moment nothing glowed within it.

"And second fireplace." We had walked right past this smaller one. Over it, hanging from a great iron hook was a large black kettle.

"For pig soup."

"Pig soup," I echoed. Abundant light shone on the kettle's watery surface.

"Anything left over makes soup *for pigs*. One fire for family food. One for pig food."

Maize cobs hung from rafters along with strands of dried meat and bouquets of herbs. Slits of sunshine patterned floor and walls. And visible to the side of the main fireplace now was another, much smaller sleeping platform perhaps eight feet square. The effect was of a sacrificial site.

"Guests sleep here . . . *your* room."

"My God," Blair said.

We were further informed that we must sleep with our heads facing the ancestral altar. Keena pointed to it, and her arm went out in a sharp diagonal sweep toward the fields. In brief: the platform, Blair and I, and the altar would be properly lined up for easy ancestral as well as in-house visibility.

We ate the quite substantial cold lunch provided by the hotel-kitchen, complete with pound cake and bottles of still cool beer which Keena refused in favor of a canned popular regional soft drink of tremendous sweetness. The low table in front of the main hearth meant cross-legged sitting—never a joy for me and an evident challenge for Blair whose left leg was still troublesome, although he had stopped the alarming limping. Every move of Keena's was as graceful as a ballerina's.

When we'd finished, all the edible remains went into the "pig pot"; everything else, in a black plastic garbage can, as alien as a space ship.

The split-bamboo irrigation system proved elegant beyond expectations and instantly engaged Blair's attention. WATER. I photographed as much of it as I reasonably could. Open lengths of large, fresh-looking bamboo lay gutter fashion, each layer tucked under the one above and meandering downhill seemingly endlessly. The whole apparatus, fashioned without joints and propped on sturdy poles, was high enough for people and animals to pass beneath. With the widest split-bamboo sections located on the highest points of land, the system is progressively bifurcated and rebifurcated as it searches out each group of houses whose fields the water must serve. Repair is ongoing. And anyone walking by can reach up to search a length of bamboo for unwanted sludge.

We were lured from my mapping to share in cups of hot tea alongside one family's fieldhouse where work had temporarily halted for some R & R. A horse with a great basket on its back was tethered with just enough leash to move about, and an unattractive chicken was pegged as a raucous sentinel both for approaching "bonus-food" in the form of a bird or small animal and for any less welcome, larger mountain predator. The crossbow and musket, propped against the fieldhouse, now made sense: a silent weapon for food, a noisy one for more fearsome prey.

But Keena's approach to guidehood essentially was to keep us moving. Blair was cooperative once he realized we were covering ground. However, it was on this point of rising cordiality that we briefly "lost" Keena . . . and inadvertently opened an unanticipated window on the Hmong world.

She had been in the process of explaining the order in which families set off and return from work: men followed by horses, followed by women (and children). The sloping land gave a fine view of valleys below. Then, suddenly, I saw a woman climbing sharply up toward us. She arrived not the least breathless, as adapted to mountains as a gazelle. When she spoke to Keena, my body went on full alert. Whatever the news it was not jolly. After a rapid exchange, Keena nodded and dispatched the messenger back down the hill. Her eyes went uncertainly to Blair and me.

"Can you find your way back to the house?"

We assured her we could, and I was struggling to conceal my elation over unsupervised time when she added:

"I will meet you there in one half hour" . . . voice and eyes archly emphatic on the *one half.* Then she started downhill, overtaking the messenger.

Ten minutes later we were prowling those areas Keena had been careful to skirt. And soon, north of anywhere we'd been, I found myself staring into what Blair assured me had once been a thriving cornfield.

"But there sure in hell isn't any corn in it now, except for a lot of stubble that any decent farmer would have done something about long ago."

I looked at him questioningly.

"I ought to know. I live in Australia, but I was raised in Iowa."

We moved in closer. With only a loosely defined fence the field was quite accessible. Poppies were now visible in various stages of wilting. Dried petals lay at our feet and in the cut, half-weeded remains of corn stalks.

"Poppies," I said, trying to make sense of it, but even as my lips formed the words my brain did the translation.

Bill Blair was faster.

"Opium!" We stepped back in tandem as though the fence were wired.

"Opium," I repeated.

Beyond and above us as we climbed were intermittent fields of it. Here was the sun, the high elevation, and the limestone soil of the frost-free Golden Triangle . . . all that opium loves. Moribund maize fields, I would learn, provide a lovely cradle for the opium seed. Once a crop is harvested, the woody leftover maize stems and a reworked soil shelter the now-planted opium seeds from seasonal rains.

And Jai had managed to program our "little adventure" in tandem with the imminent incision of the opium heads (or bulbs) and the careful collection of their sap-like bounty. And *that* explained the xenophobic paranoia of the driver, the community, and the tribal center.

"Rice for the belly; opium for the pocket" was the way it was later explained to me. Opium was the Hmong's cash crop,[2] sold for the *sure*, redeemable insurance of silver (the preferred payment medium) . . . and relegated to the safety, not of banks, but of hiding places (sometimes subterranean) in locked houses such as the one in which we were to spend the night.

Blair looked at his watch. "Time to head back."

"My thoughts exactly." We were beginning to think in tandem.

"Just as soon not be found here although we're probably the only ones north of Chiang Mai to whom the opium would come as a surprise."

My hand was on my pocket and the camera. But then I shook my head and Blair nodded his approval.

"I don't fancy a bamboo-knuckle manicure for either of us."

We were within a hundred yards of the house, back on what was now familiar trail, when Keena reappeared, moving fast.

"We have had word from your family," she said without preamble, eyes focused on Blair. "Your wife has given birth."

No sound emerged from Blair.

"It has taken a day to trace you since everyone thought you were in Bangkok. But your last credit card charge was from the Chiang Mai hotel, and they were very cooperative. . . . Anyway, you have a son. I am to tell you that he is fine and so is his mother and you are not to worry about them."

"A son." The words were mine. It took Blair several more seconds before he could repeat them.

The message had come via battery-operated radio, located God knows where, and Keena had communicated that we would be returning to Chiang Mai forthwith. That had required alerting a driver to pick us up at the point we had been deposited. The window of opportunity, we were told, lasted only until nightfall because the trails were not safe after dark. Mentally I filled in the blanks: sizable animals and/or drug caravans.

As a second order of consideration, we must return to "our house." Good form dictated that we take our leave somewhat ceremoniously. Clearly, Keena did not wish to compromise her continuing good standing with the hill people, which was fair enough.

We walked into the beginning of what proved to be a celebration, with the headman returning from the fields early for it. Also on hand were his wife (whom we'd met), their three children, and two neighbors.

Keena explained what the excitement was about. The Hmong are polygynous. A woman can have only one husband, but a man can have any number of wives. All wives live under the same roof and are entitled to share the "husband's bed," but in the separate sleeping platforms we had seen. Polygyny is possible only for the wealthy since bride-price is high.

"Mr. Blair's taking a *second* wife and his first wife giving him a son. . . . Only a superior man is able to take on the responsibilities of both. It calls for a celebration."

Blair was beaming.

Keena went on. "But it also calls for an acknowledgment to the spirits that we are grateful for their power to bring such treasured events."

The best course of action, she emphasized, was for us to go along. "Anything less would be unwise."

To Bill Blair fell the special honor of sharing an opium "lamp"—refusal of which would be a shabby response to their concern for him, his son, and his respective wives. The narcotic content, Keena assured us, was comparatively low, given the semicooked state of the opium.

It was almost five o'clock when we started our trek back up the hills. All in all, not a bad resolution to the day. Neither of us was unhappy about skipping our night's accommodation. I *was* worried that Blair's still ailing leg might actually risk stranding us on the trail into the twilight hours. But he moved along with surprising alacrity.

"Better than I thought," he said, stroking the leg. "Better than it has been. Practically no pain at all."

"The opium!" Keena announced, not missing a step, her voice rolling out across the nests of twisted trees and orchids newly radiant in the slanting sunlight. "It is the effect of the opium."

Blair turned to stare at me and shrugged his shoulders as she continued her medical evaluation.

"Opium is especially prized for the aches and pains and injuries of *old age*."

The driver had returned to where we left him and was now an endearing sight.

Back at the hotel, Jai was nowhere to be seen. Blair headed for his room and a phone. Dirty as I was, I decided to get some food and a drink before I headed for the longest shower on record. I walked to the dining room and pulled open its stately doors.

And there, in that sizable restaurant, where no more than twenty of us had been served at breakfast, was an expanse of uniformed men and officers of the United States Air Force. They filled three tables and two booths near the entrance. The sight of them was so unexpected that I stood riveted in the doorway... as whatever reservations I'd had on U.S. interest in Chiang Mai vanished like water down an unplugged drain.

Their presence dominated the place. In the seconds I stood weighing the strategy of weaving past them to the otherwise thinly occupied room, several hands went up in waves of greeting. And—in the not-uncommon bond that links obvious "outsiders" in less-traveled areas of the world—I was invited to join a table.

The men were gracious, studiously polite, and in no time at all had negotiated an extra dinner plate for me and were guiding me through food choices from bowls still hot with food. They knew the waiter by name and were soon promoting more to drink . . . with the added insistence on brand name.

"You have to watch it around here," one of them offered. "The hotel is pretty much first-rate and they take good care of us . . . but, in these parts, nothing's ever easy."

Heads nodded in agreement, launching laughter and stories of their gradual and joint initiation into life Chiang Mai–style.

Clearly they were no strangers to the area and while I was mentally wrestling with a reasonable approach as to *why . . .* they put the question to me. What was *I* doing in Chiang Mai?

I was candid, if brief, about my interest in the hill country. I ran through my problems finding a guide and Jai's initiative in providing one for me. And I was weighing how to proceed when the next question came.

"Jai sent you into hill country?"

"It was *my* idea."

"Where'd you go?"

"North and east. A scheduled overnight. But . . ."

Someone else plunged in.

"You *overnighted* in the Hmong hills?"

"No . . . no. It didn't work out . . . I came back. Just now actually." I gestured toward my clothes; they looked more than a little well traveled.

"That damn Jai." Another voice was contributing. "He'd send his mother to a vampire's picnic."

The men were looking at one another now in an obvious consensus and, after a few seconds' lull, the captain (and apparent "spokesperson") put down his glass.

"I hope you're not planning any more hill-country excursions."

I shook my head. "I'm due elsewhere."

"Good!"

Heads nodded, and the men began to tackle the food again, by which time I concluded that it was fair enough for me to put the question to them.

"What are you fellows doing in Chiang Mai?"

No one missed a stroke except for the captain—the single officer at the table.

"We're a presence," he said.

"What does *that* mean?"

"Anything the U.S. military wants it to mean." His voice was amiable; his demeanor unchanged. "And pass the rice, will you?"

He gave me a slow smile. I met his smile and passed the rice.

Notes

[1] Despite denials, there is reputed to have been some degree of help—however derived—from the United States Central Intelligence Agency and a CIA-controlled airline. See Neil and Susan Sheehan, "A Reporter at Large in Vietnam," *The New Yorker*, November 18, 1991.

[2] The Hmong themselves use opium very discriminately if at all, and principally for medical or ceremonial reasons or the comfort of respected older kinsmen or guests.

5

The Enculturation Process
How French Children Learn to Drink

The anthropologist does not have to be in a brand-new community very long before experiencing some selective rush of memories. For me, the challenge of a new language, whatever my preparation, evokes Benjamin Franklin's lamentation upon his arrival in Paris as ambassador and spokesperson for the young United States that "even the little children speak French." More than once I have found myself pressing one of my children for words that were commonplace in their vocabularies while, after months of residence, I clung to a pocket dictionary—just in case.

With disturbing regularity I would envy all children the ongoing enculturation process, so bleakly denied me. Parents, siblings, their age-mates, not to mention *teachers* band together—on all fronts—helping the child develop a very special cultural rationality. Even the ready, unapologetic sanctions that are brought to bear on children's mistakes are more often than not empathetic . . . directed to a promised, shining, shared goal of optimal functioning within the world in which they daily move.

The appeal for cultural entry or credentials *as an adult*, on the other hand, brings dismay to those around one. The timing is wrong. One has missed the boat. That lovely syncopated pattern of living, jointly achieved, no longer yields to easy translation. It's like trying to read backwards.

As anthropologists, what most of us hope for is some vicarious, if tardy, reconstruction of the enculturative process. Fieldwork demands it. Our academic training will, we hope, have been geared to some general reservoir of knowledge about the culture within which we struggle for insights as we respond to the not-so-simple demands of daily living. But what we lack in terms of the secure roots of early enculturation we must try, however modestly, to compensate for if we are ever to achieve any field acceptance *or* sensibility.

The French are not alone among the world's peoples in regarding their learned way of life as emulable. And while I was in France, with my anthropologist husband and two daughters (ages seven and two), wrapping up almost two years of work in the village of Vertier, I was witness to a development that would help me understand the dynamics of cultural consensus and the factors that contribute to its persistence. In this case, the subject was the French dedication to wine drinking.

Visitors to France—even those with some knowledge of Mediterranean cultures—are often startled by the great amount of wine drinking they find. The French, everywhere, drink with unflagging dedication and a quiet passion.

But now, the country's Institute of Public Opinion was taking on the awesome task of altering France's drinking habits. In anthropological terms, this amounted to an analysis of patterns of enculturation to wine drinking.

A significant portion of the French population was, on a daily basis, imbibing considerably more than the judicious glass or two of red wine, whose intake had been applauded as therapeutic in some medical contexts. Indeed 15 percent of France's inhabitants were considered "alcoholics," with another 30 percent consuming alcohol in amounts incontrovertibly dangerous to their health. Additionally industrial-accident figures were mounting, as were speculations as to the relationship between intoxication and the quality of family life.

Our village was to prove fairly representative of France, wherein the total annual consumption of *pure alcohol* had reached 32 quarts per adult, which was within one quart of *doubling* the intake of the world's second largest wine-consuming country—Italy. Yet for the average French man or woman, alcoholism, we knew, is identified only with reeling drunkenness.

The energies of various agencies of the French government (for whom the consequences of alcoholism were costly as well as dismaying) were being marshalled to put some brakes on alcoholic intake and to encourage the development of alternative drinking patterns, particularly in the emerging generation.

As it happened, I was already well involved in making sense of the overall eating patterns within Vertier. These had meaning, we had come to realize, in solidifying familial togetherness as well as formalizing village judgments about a vast range of social activities. My being offered a glass of wine in the context of a home visit, for example, sent the message of my acceptance by the family—a green light in terms of the privilege of continuing access to their home. And I regarded it as no mean achievement. Without this gesture I hadn't a chance at periodic interviewing, since it was rarely sensible otherwise to take on the challenge of getting to the front door unexpected or unwanted. In three out of four homes one faced the common triad of cement-and-iron-fenced enclosures, a noisy rock-strewn path (that made your footsteps heard), and the leashed but vicious dog chained within range of the entrance.

Over the months, as anthropologists, we gradually moved from an alien presence to a largely innocuous part of the community. What we did was neither laudatory nor alarming. Eccentric was perhaps closer to the nature of our interests as we came to participate in village life and, to the extent possible, penetrated behind the scenes. Our children marshalled vastly more caring attention, given the burden they clearly faced with parents who needed to be guided through some of the most basic tenets of child care. The birth of our third child during our residence sent off real alarms, and I was able to get a long-sought housekeeper in the person of Madame Cluny (herself the mother of ten grown children) essentially to make sure that the rudiments of proper infant care—including a modified form of swaddling[1]—were not denied this newest "villager." My status did get a boost, however, when the news got about that I was nursing our new son. Word had it that American women were rarely so inclined and even when so disposed were seldom sufficiently endowed to do the job.

I had developed and put to use a questionnaire on family life in general, and now I extended it to include a section on what every member of a household had eaten or had to drink in the past 24 hours—at home or away from home. Of huge help was the increasingly evident village concern that our children be properly guided in terms of the nutritional and gastronomic resources of French food.

Also, I had stumbled across some of the plastic reproductions of food and serving dishes with which children "play house," including replicas of the drinking glasses most in use in Vertier. I could now better quantify the data I was collecting. If someone had had a steak at lunch, I could point to a replica and ask: "Big as this? . . . Smaller?" Among my collection was a plastic rendering of french-fried potatoes that made just about everyone laugh, because they did not remotely approach the appeal of the crispy and steamy "pommes frites" appreciated by local cooks. But there was little doubt that the wine glasses, varying significantly as they did in size, gave realistic documentation of cumulative daily intake.

My use of the latter found me seriously struggling with the ethical ramifications of my interest in the government's concern regarding alcoholism. But neither the men nor the women were distressed when I shared with them the government's interest in their behavior, although they *did* interpret the undertaking negatively—but for reasons I had *not* anticipated. What they wanted me to know (and the government too for that matter) was that they could read the handwriting on the wall: the goal of all this was not some sudden humanitarian commitment on the part of officialdom to a shared sobriety. Some shook their heads at my naiveté.

No, indeed. This was a governmental prelude to a program of "taxation increase" on wine, one of the simple but persisting pleasures of France's already over-taxed working families everywhere. These "reformers" (more laughter), given their elevated incomes, were in all likelihood drinking as much, if not more—and better—wine.

They were not concerned about the collection of information that was surely already known at all levels of government.

More avidly invested in the outcome of all this was the country's powerful *wine lobby*, which had promptly mounted a full-scale campaign repudiating all claims as to wine's less-than-laudatory role in the daily lives and health of France's men, women, and *children*.

They showed a shrewd recognition of the early roots of wine appreciation. In Vertier's elementary school rooms, for example, the extraordinarily active wine lobby distributed *blotters* (in early classes French children were encouraged to write with pens and inkwells) asserting that a liter of wine (12 percent alcohol) has nutritive value equivalent to 850 grams of milk, 370 grams of bread, 585 grams of meat or 5 eggs. The blotter had a drawing of a scale with a wine bottle balancing these foods.

This posture, it needs to be made clear, was congenial to the positive value in the food chain which many Frenchmen regarded as attaching to wine. As a product of sun-drenched grapes, nurtured to ripeness in the rich soil of France, wine is seen as a laudable time-tested contribution to well-being, fulfilling much the same role as vitamins—*and* less artificially. Wine is also believed to be helpful in the demanding lives of manual workers. The body can best endure muscular exertion, some alleged, with the sustained, revitalizing support of wine. Strong men have a propensity for drink. It is nature's way—"C'est comme ça."

Finally, wine may not be purer then any other drink, but most villagers think it is. In fact, the alcohol in wine was widely believed to compensate for the unsanitary conditions under which it, and many other food products, are prepared.

All these beliefs were strongest among those who worked Vertier's land or were in related occupations. The few upper-middle-class families also linked wine drinking to vigor. But they were more likely to stress moderation and did drink less wine. However, this comparative discretion apparently did not extend to *aperitifs* and *digestifs*, of which they drank considerably more both at home and in cafés.

In contrast with the positive value placed on wine, our Frenchmen placed a negative value on two major *non*alcoholic drinks: water and milk. For one thing, Vertier's spring-water fountains located in key areas of the community had long been subject to *taxation* by the government! However, the wily villagers posted signs onto the fountains reading NON-POTABLE or UNDRINKABLE and so got away with their infrequent use of them since it was a rare household that was without some fauceted source of water. It was a long time before I discovered the "secret" of the available and superior-tasting spring-water supply.

In any case, little water was drunk (except in coffee), especially by the men. The local attitude is that, although a certain amount of consumption is inevitable, water takes second place to almost any other beverage. As one of the huge wine lobby's subway signs put it: "Water is for frogs."

In its campaign against the wine lobby, the French government turned to building the image of fruit juice. Government ads proliferated on subway walls, billboards, and in magazines showing sweaty popular sportsmen downing a can of juice with apparent gusto. Villagers were unmoved. Canned beverages of any kind were Vertier's most expensive beverage—wildly so.

As for milk, a precept firmly adhered to and advocated in many of the well-thumbed, time-tested books on child care was summed up in one of these: "Milk should never constitute the regular mealtime drink." The risk apparently is of digestive troubles such as diarrhea. When children stopped taking the breast or the bottle and eating the *bouillies* (thin milk mushes) of babyhood, they rarely drank milk except in *café au lait*, hot chocolate, or the milk-thinned mashed vegetables called *purées*.

Of course, in all fairness, the fact that milk was generally inadequately refrigerated—even in stores—added nothing to its appeal, especially in warm weather when it could take on a strong, almost curdled flavor.

On the other hand, commitment to wine drinking often begins very early in life. And government efforts to show that wine hurts children run into a semantic trap. A child does not drink wine; he or she drinks "reddened water."

For our villagers the consumption of wine in a daily intake of less than a quarter of a liter was equivalent to abstinence. The mother of a boy of twelve assured me that her son did not drink at all, though the boy sat across from me at the table with a glass of highly diluted wine in his hand. By this, she meant that his "reddened water" contained only a couple of soupspoons of wine, an amount too negligible for recognition.

Of huge help in identifying families' vision of their own and their children's food and drink commitments was the spreading concern that my children be properly guided in terms of the gastronomic resources of French food, even though it had become evident they would be denied the appropriate introduction to French wines. In one morale-shattering incident, our Katie had coughed out the first swallow of a glass of water with wine so "thinned" that the color had not signaled its contents.

On a visit to nearby Antony, I bought refreshments for my daughter and her 11-year-old playmate, at a cafe. The girl ordered and drank a bottle of beer. It surprised me because her mother had told me that the girl did not drink. But I am sure that, to the mother, her child's minimal and irregular intake did not constitute *drinking*.

It was not unusual to see a toddler take a sip of beer or cider, as well as wine, from a parent's glass. And as boys and girls get older and more demanding, they may occasionally be given quite small glasses of their own. Children of farm and working-class families, who predominated in Vertier, drank more and started earlier than children of middle-class families. One mother even reported putting a drop or two of wine in the baby's bottle to "fortify" the milk. But generally wine is first offered when the child can hold a glass quite safely in hand and join the family at table.

In short, wine drinking has long been a part of the scenario of the good life, its virtues communicated well before French children are old enough to reflect about it. If they—or their parents—should begin to assess their drinking practices, as the government was asking them to do, it would be against a cultural backdrop where all the answers are value-loaded. Under the circumstances, it was hardly surprising that the alcohol reduction campaign in France met with little success and that the wine-drinking patterns of French villagers in particular changed virtually not at all—despite the government's valiant health message.

I remember the yearlong undertaking as a testament to the often seamless power of the enculturation process, whatever one's judgment of it.

For the field anthropologist the dynamics of enculturation are initially invisible. Even with the most earnest and
well-guided preparation for a particular culture, the uncover-
ing of the *taken-for-granted* in the lives of the people we study
is very demanding business. It's a little like having mastered a
static image of the heart and its functions without ever having
ventured into examination of an actual specimen of one—let
alone a breathing, life-sustaining one.

To some extent, every culture takes on a common "vitality." What has given it that vitality, that *life*, is what the cultural anthropologist pledges most of his or her professional
energies to comprehend—at least to the extent that involvement in that life and informed reflection upon it make possible. Our efforts draw upon all that we have learned (and need
continuously to learn).

In the case of cultures, unlike the human heart, definitions of "normalcy" have a huge, seemingly limitless range.
Yet, within cultures, there are common generating systems at
work. Like the French, all people eat and drink. What they
prize or avoid as food or drink, ignore or pay highly for in cur-
rency or energy: these differ between cultures. The underlying
value system that sustains (or alters) these priorities is a
learned one. Much of it learned early.

Everywhere the process of enculturation is in motion
long before any underlying rationale can be weighed independent of a preestablished consensus. And—much as with food
and drink—social organization, political ideals and prejudices,
what is or is not to be appreciated as a laudable work of art,
and what is worth the selective investment of personal and
familial resources—even the *definition* of family: all these, and
more, are molded over the months and years of early life into
a formula for living. Preferably living well. Even in the shaping of alternative goals, revolutionists are influenced by the
consensus they choose to alter.

In the field the anthropologist to some extent aspires to
the role of "stand-in" for the ongoing drama of the encultura-

tive process. In Vertier I would find myself wondering: "What is this mother going to do next? Is she going to offer him a bit of her cider? Will she be intimidated by my presence, or will I get to see it all played out as usual? What is going on in her mind when she hands that glass to that toddler to sip; what process of motivation would incline me to identify—more positively than I now can—with her convictions and the obvious regularity of such actions?" In brief: how can I take on the worldview, the mental map, the formula for loving child care that is embodied in this woman before me—this French village mother.

It is not difficult for anthropologists to find themselves judgmental. But this posture can too easily get in the way of a necessary "appreciation" of what underlies the status quo. This appreciation is especially crucial to the success of applied fieldwork. If any alteration in existing patterns of behavior is to take root, the dynamics that sustain them must be recognized in their effectiveness.

The failure of the French campaign to alter the drinking practices of an emerging generation followed from an understandable, but unfortunate reluctance or inability to jump-start the campaign from the perspective of existing "drinkers."

Note

[1] The "swaddled" infant is a wrapped infant. In some cultures this involves wrapping the baby's entire body. Uncontrolled thrashing about, it is feared, might well bring bodily harm in the form of broken or dislocated bones. Another concern is that the baby's legs grow straight. Vertier's version of swaddling was a gentle one: a length of cloth, folded envelope-fashion and anchored to the baby's diaper, restricted but did not notably inhibit leg movement.

PSYCHOLOGICAL ANTHROPOLOGY

6

The Self and Others
The Shaping of Shame in Morocco

Some cultures simply make life more challenging than others for the roaming anthropologist. I give the Arab world three stars on "challenge," though in fairness I must add the significant modifier that I was unprepared for work within it.

Actually unfamiliarity was a criterion for my assignment to Morocco. The United States and Moroccan governments were jointly sponsoring a series of programs designed to enhance faculty areal specialization in Africa-north-of-the-Sahara. Much of the northern Mediterranean was familiar to me, but I knew little of the Arab world. I applied for and was fortunate to receive a grant for an academic year in Morocco.

Morocco is part of Africa's far west, also dubbed its Wild West. Extending as close to America as Europe's most westerly coastline, it is part of the *Maghrib*, Land of the Sunset. "Algeria is a man," the Arabs say, "Tunisia a woman, Morocco a lion." And, in 1971, Lord Kinross echoed his own enthusiasm for "a lion of a country if ever there was one."[1]

Beyond the provision of a base of operations at Mohammed V University in Rabat, the country's capital, I was to work independently (which itself would prove a problem), moving as widely around Morocco as consonant with progressive insight into Arab culture.

A half-century ago, H. A. H. Gibb ventured a brief but cogent definition of the Arab. "All those are Arabs," he wrote, "for whom the central fact of history is the mission of Muhammed and the memory of the Arab Empire and who in addition cherish the Arab tongue and its cultural heritage as their common possession."[2]

My initial fieldwork lasted eight months. Later I would manage two more visits, brief and ten years apart. Chance and opportune travel have also taken me into Algeria, Tunisia, northern Egypt, and to Bahrain on the Persian Gulf. Arabs, I would learn, do indeed share a common fund of religious, social, and intellectual convictions, although these are often regionally suspended in changing currents of emphasis. Specific populations vary in levels of sensitivity and comfort with those around them, within their borders, or beyond them—Arab or not.

And, if one is to enjoy a social posture other than that of sacrificial tourist, the stranger to the Arab world, the "outsider," must appreciate that the Arab brings to every social encounter a sense of self not easily read nor comprehended by the uninitiated.

The *self*, cross-culturally, has evaded easy interpretation by anthropologists. Much of current literature is consumed with questions about its nature and the "accessibility" of *self* to anthropological analysis.

Essentially the *self* is envisaged in a number of ways. You can think of the self as a master response mechanism, a pattern maker to which the individual, anywhere and everywhere, has been conditioned from birth. The "pattern" analogy can not be pushed too far, however, because its underlying form or constitution has to remain loose or undifferentiated enough to be put to multiple uses and shaped to various needs. Further, a culturally sharable "self" must come to terms with whatever differentiating genetic or temperamental influences become operative across the life span. Essentially, within a particular culture, it must allow more people to be valued than rejected.

Put another way, some integrity of self must be promoted as desirable: a touchstone of self-measurement. *As an ideal* this consensus amounts to a form of cultural insurance. Life will go on, it promises, under a code of behavior more often endorsed than violated.

Much of the training of cultural anthropologists involves the flexibility of mind that fieldwork demands. But sensitivity to the communication systems of *self* is demanding business, even within one's own culture. In the case of Morocco I was an impatient learner, as this chapter will attest. Much of Arab life baffled or frustrated me. I found myself judgmental, often defensive—postures which neither intellectually nor emotionally advance the course of insight. Full comprehension was perhaps never mine.

Although clues were plentiful enough, I needed help in reading them. Fortunately I would find it.

The time was the early seventies. Morocco had gained independence from France in 1956, a circumstance that left the country both passionately proud and awash still in much border-to-border bureaucratic disarray. Nor was it helpful that the "exploratory" goals expressed in my grant description proved unsettling to several agencies within the Moroccan government. With what I would later recognize as characteristic evasion, no agency had chosen to provide written authorization of my university attachment in Rabat. In the Moroccan scheme of things there is awesome vulnerability as well as privilege in responsibility. No action is better than potentially wrong (i.e., self-incriminating) action . . . a posture that applies to groups as well as to individuals.

In my case the unsatisfactory governmental resolution was that, on arrival, I should present myself to the American consulate where, ostensibly, all supporting paperwork would then be waiting for me.

I had left my children (and car) in France pending information as to where and how we might be housed and what if anything should be expected of me at Mohammed V University. My husband was winding up a semester of teaching.

When I got off the plane in Rabat, I walked into pandemonium. All I could think was that I'd been fool enough to come on some holiday or religious festival toward whose celebration whole families seemed to be departing. I walked two blocks before waving down a cab.

The driver spoke a heavily accented French.

"What's going on?" I asked him. "Looks like a revolution."

His arm went over the back seat as he turned to stare at me. "Please Madame. 'Revolution' is unwise talk. There has been an attempt on the life of our illustrious monarch."

"Hassan? . . . Hassan II, the *king*?"

"He is unharmed. It is said his bodyguards pulled him from under the fallen bodies of the less fortunate, gunned down all of them at a luncheon at the palace."

The car was weaving in and out of traffic as though the driver's vision—fixed on me—were superfluous and the car governed by radar.

"The road!" I yelled.

"It was a miracle." Again his hands left the wheel, this time to be joined in a position of prayer. "Allah was watching over him . . . I am told that any man within a block of the palace was imprisoned or shot. There is talk of a coup."

His was the first of a stream of fanciful accounts of whatever occurred. There was never consensus. More relevantly for me, the academic department to which I was to report had been "dissolved." The cultural attaché of the American Consulate explained it to me when I appeared at her office seeking guidance. Apparently no one within the government had *ever* been fervent about a university department that, despite some commendable ethnological efforts, probed issues of social change.

"Change," she assured me "has a more sinister ring in the throne room than in the classroom."

She was the calmest person I would run into in the city. And within 48 hours I was back in her office to be informed that I should now be accommodated in the foreign language division of the university, within which all features of my grant would be honored . . . except that, for the foreseeable future, I could not leave Rabat.

"*What?*" How could I work and not leave Rabat? And what about all those people at the airport? They were leaving in droves.

She elaborated. I could leave the country. Go home. But in all likelihood I would not be permitted to reenter or to travel within Morocco without a newly proposed "visa," the scope of which was yet to be defined . . . subject perhaps to presentation at checkpoints or on demand.

I was devastated. Thus far, in Morocco, incredulity seemed to be my permanent state of mind.

But the attaché just shrugged. "In a few weeks time, less probably, it will all blow over and things will be back to normal. One thing *is* predictable. None of these measures will prove particularly efficient . . . and there are always those who know how to work the system."

So there was nothing to do but wait it out. And sure enough, the tumult subsided almost as swiftly as it had begun. In less than a week Hassan was making public appearances. Travel was feasible but not recommended. I flew back to Paris and with two children drove across France and Spain in our little red Renault, ferried the Straits of Gibraltar into Tangiers, and drove into Morocco.

During the wild exodus from Rabat I had rented an attractive apartment from a nervous landlord fearful of an empty building. As a kind of bonus, "Amina," a cleaning woman, and sometimes maid, came with the place. The accommodations, thoroughly Arabic in character, included a central patio. The die had been cast. I was headquartered in the capital. Time in Rabat could be put to good use, and the university provided a place for much-needed research. My colleagues were friendly and unruffled. I began some one-on-one intensive lessons in spoken Arabic.

That I managed over time to get anything done in Morocco I credit, in particular, to three individuals who kept me functioning with minimal havoc. They proved critical guides. One was American, one French, one Moroccan. Something in the mix was therapeutic, for on all these cultural levels Morocco and I were intermittently in and out of some level of synchronization.

The American cultural attaché became an ongoing mentor until her transfer about halfway through my stay. I mourned the loss. From her I learned when to *confront* major obstacles and how.

From the second "guide," a retired French physician who lived in our building, I was ingenuously tutored on how to *accept* aggravations or, as he put it, when to go with the established flow and how.

But the gap between education and action was sometimes wide. And when in doubt as to strategies I sometimes sought the counsel of my third resource: Abdul, who had a shoe repair shop in the *medina* (literally 'city' in Arabic), the native quarter, set off by walls and gates from the central European city that had grown up outside it. My home was about four long blocks from the medina. Abdul also managed the operations of a fleet of shoe-shine boys who roamed the terraces of hotels and major squares of Rabat. He was unusual in having spent four years of his life in the United States. His wife's family owned a rug emporium in Fez.

I had status with Abdul. More by reflex action than heroism, I had snatched his nephew (a shoe-shine boy) out of the way of a car door that shot open as a battered vehicle careened around a curve on one of Rabat's main streets. I suffered a few black-and-blue marks that vanished in a week or two. But Abdul and his family "owed" me.

I express this "owing" in the sense that Abdul understood it, which involved considerable debt. In the Arab world the most lavish verbal expression of thanks for a service rendered is rarely enough. "Do not thank me. You will repay me," was an expression that initially shocked me. I heard it often. My French physician friend "translated" for me: "You will repay me . . . not necessarily tomorrow or at the next encounter, but . . . 'the marker' is out."

"Marker?" It sounded like a gambling debt and I said so.

"Right! And everyone keeps track of what he owes and what is owing him. It's beneficial, actually. Keeps assets circulating."

He had a quick example.

"A woman knows that, having—unasked—cooked and brought food to a neighbor's wedding celebration, an event always swamped with guests, she need not fret about an ample enough feast when sometime in the future her resources are similarly challenged. Her neighbor will provide. She *owes* her. They will each know when it's time to offer or collect."

Moroccan life, I would learn, is quite literally a balance sheet of give and take. Consensus and cohesion make the system work in a vast scope of predictable interdependency. Socially and cognitively, Moroccan households, workplaces, diversion areas are shared terrains, pieces of some gigantic jigsaw puzzle that never reaches completion. The American concept of privacy, of inviolableness, or a free-standing "me" is alien to the Moroccan concept of self.

This social equation was hard going for me. I found myself, for example, avoiding certain sections of the medina because of Abdul, who felt socially corrupted in not finding singular ways of responding to my "having saved his nephew's life," particularly since my conscience would not allow me to accept the gift of a rug of great value. He was relentless in his promises that he would be there for me if I should need him. And *that*, I assured him, was the most precious gift of all. In the medina I was known as "Abdul's friend," and when I passed the open shops heads nodded in recognition and there were smiles. I was not hassled.

Yet as the days passed the "mechanics" of Arab interaction were troubling. I was having difficulty learning how to translate the expectations of others as these affected the daily routines I was trying hard to establish. Privileges and obligations colored a distracting number of activities. Nothing seemed simply to "flow" of its own independent stimulus.

The product of all this obsessive togetherness was not contributing to a very secure *me*.

One morning I came downstairs to find my car's radio antenna tied in a graceful loop. My apartment had come with a designated sidewalk parking space that simplified life and saved time. But now . . . vandalism! I checked my tires and the body of the car. Everything else was fine.

A boy about eight or nine who seemed always underfoot was smiling at me with contrived shyness. I knew him. He always had his hand out, but I'd soon tired of putting spare coins in it, encouraging his hanging about . . . and now he'd gotten even! But I hadn't seen him do it. That evening I vented my disillusionment on Dr. Girard, my French physician neighbor and counselor. He was taking the air as usual on the balcony adjoining mine.

"Well, my dear woman," he said, "you've obviously fallen seriously in arrears in your payments. That's Mohammed, sending you an overdue notice."

"Payments! For what? He's not entitled to a dime."

"*Dirham*," Dr. Girard corrected. . . . "No. No. You must think of him as your watchman, caretaker, policeman."

"Self-selected vandal."

"It's distressing, of course. But not irreparable. And you must learn to give credit where credit is due. In a tough world Mohammed has carved out a modest business for himself. He's quite an enterprising young fellow. Think of Mohammed as your car's overseer. And remember, besides the fact that your car will be protected from the loss or damage of critical parts or gasoline, Mohammed offers other benefits. In an emergency, and for just a few extra *dirhams* he can get a message for you to just about any local shop or house, and his old grandmother will do mending for you if you need it. Very ably too. She turns the cuffs on my shirts at a price I couldn't replicate anywhere."

"Why in the world didn't he say something?"

"Because you were supposed to have gotten the message!"

We both laughed and I stopped whining.

"Well, what am I supposed to give him?"

"The rate is fixed . . . and for heaven's sake don't get yourself into hassling it. Don't ask. Your asking him now means opening up what should have been a *done deal* on price."

"And how was I supposed to know that?"

"You ask someone who deals with the same obligation, like me."

Thereafter, every morning as I pulled away from the curb I dropped the designated number of dirhams into Mohammed's discreetly cupped hand. My radio antenna was promptly restored to pristine condition.

"His older brother's a mechanic's helper," Dr. Girard later elaborated. "And listen . . . if once in a while the boy renders a particular service—points out a spongy tire, wipes a really dirty windshield or just because the sun is shining and you feel good about the world—you can give him something extra. It will give him status. He won't overdo, or I'll get after him. He's a good boy. And we do need him."

He was right, of course, and it worked. And it was becoming disturbingly evident that the major problem in most of these impasses lay within me. Not out there in some free-standing cultureless "right" and "wrong." I had appreciated cultural differences well enough to undertake intensive study of the Arab language but managed to remain far less compulsive about the equally complex lexicon of Arab behavior, just as old a cultural commodity.

I was spending my days reading "conscience" into a world whose integrity translated in terms of "shame."

The control factor in all this is the presence of a vigilant viewer, "an audience." In the case of my car the combined apartment house membership with its old Morocco hands precluded abuse of an established and mutually fruitful contract. A greedy or derelict Mohammed would be *shamed* by them, but more grievously, by his own family, extended members of which would no longer profit from his connection.

Clearly, it behooved me to make the move from "outsider" (unprotected) to "insider" (protected) with all the rights and obligations pertaining to that status. It was the way to go.

The codebook for social incorporation into Arab life was opening to me. Within the limited Morocco of which I was now becoming a part, social mobility and social definition were best accessed on the broadest screen of actors involved in my daily life. And somewhere within that cultural screen also lay the definition of peace, progress, and power.

The Arab self, I was learning, is distinguished by an internal code very different from the American code. It embodies a different consensus about the roots of self-image, about the proper presentation of self, about what to do and what to avoid toward the achievement of self-enhancement and social advantage.

The shared logic and cohesion of all this, almost by definition, is foreign to the outsider. To the Arab it is as automatic
as breathing and virtually as little questioned.

A relevant experience comes to mind.

Weeks had passed, and I had settled into a better tempo
of research, fieldwork, and travel through Morocco. Often the
children traveled with me; their school calendar was riddled
with holidays. And when they went off to a "colonie de vacan-
ces" with their former French classmates, I ventured into
longer travel commitments.

Yet even as my contacts and freedom expanded, one
dimension of life remained aggravating and sometimes inhib-
iting. Strangers and friends, even Abdul's eight-year-old
nephew, were forever asking some version of "Where is your
man?"

To move so freely about the city and medina, to head a
household with children, and to drive alone to places like Taza,
Oulmès or Taroudannt, or to Marrakech on the fringe of the
Sahara: these were things few women, even European, did
without a man. Further, my interests mountingly involved me
in social contexts within which Arab women rarely if ever
sought engagement . . . "*Where* was my man?"

I went to see Abdul in the medina. He sent his small assistant off for fresh mint and prepared the sweet, fragrant tea I
had come to like. Especially I enjoyed watching the practiced
sweep of the teapot as he lowered its spout, then drew it back
to create a great arc, and the pale green liquid spun unerringly
across two or three feet of space into the minute oval of a cup.

After a prescribed interval of appreciative verbal
exchanges (one *never* plunges into the topic that really has
brought one), I got to the point of my visit. Abdul, as usual,
went to the heart of the matter.

"But of course there must always be a *man*," he said.

"Abdul, it will be weeks before my husband can join me."

"I perhaps have not been clear. There must always be a
man . . . in the next room, about to appear, delayed at his office
in the very important work that is demanded of him. Another

male relative. An Arab friend. Me! Some man. Expected. Near. In a position to be very unhappy about anything untoward, unkind, threatening that might occur to you. An American colleague, statesman—if it comes to that . . . But no, no. For the most part it is just the posture, the communication of power. Always confident! That is important."

He blinked an additional message with the odd combination of humor and sobriety that he affected.

"Never, never do we want some sorry conclusion drawn as to your vulnerability . . . or availability."

And then, to clear the air, he chastised his little helper about the limited supply of fresh mint and the boy was off again.

But I shook my head. "Thank you, Abdul. I must decline more tea. But your hospitality once again is the most gracious in all of Rabat." And I thanked him for his advice.

"Of course you did not hear it from me," he said as we parted.

It was in the context of my getting stranded "manless" in a town on the western slope of the Middle Atlas mountains that I learned the wisdom of Abdul's counsel and went native in terms of gender-based expectations.

Moroccans get around on everything from planes to camels, but one thing I had found even less welcome than a camel ride was a trip on a really local bus. And I avoided them. My last, pre-Renault experience had been a bus ride made memorable only in its abjectness. We were double capacity in passengers, in addition to which several chickens were miserably tied to the roof from which their cries and feathers floated through the paneless windows. The boy beside me had the worst time of it, throwing up intermittently between his legs.

But now, in the hill town, my Renault began lunging about at slower and slower speeds until it was clear I had a major problem on my hands. I found a garage with a mechanic who spoke with impressive knowledgeability about what needed to be done. The parts must be sent for. In three or four days I could have my car.

There was, I learned, a local car-rental agency. Great. I could use the time to go to Essaouira, a Portuguese-founded town and fishing center on the coast and perhaps on to lively Agadir, wholly rebuilt after a devastating earthquake.

Yes, I would rent a car.

The agency was not large. They had a car and, yes, four days would be feasible. But it was as the clerk pulled out a contract form that I became aware of a new note . . . of hesitation. He looked beyond me toward the door and then over his shoulder where, through the window behind him, the car lot was visible. When the question came, I was ready for it.

"Where is your man?" he asked, as though my male companion had somehow managed to get lost on the premises.

"My husband is at the hotel."

"He must sign for the car."

"Of course," I agreed. "May I show him the form? It will go faster."

A second or two went by during which I kept my eyes locked on his. Then with evident displeasure the clerk peeled off the single-sheet contract from a gummed pad of them.

I left and treated myself to lunch.

At 2:30 I returned to the agency having completed the rental form myself and then, with a separate, broad-pointed pen, signed my husband's name in bold script.

But the game, I knew, was far from over. And sure enough, after I placed the contract in his hands, the man stared at me with impatience. He was not happy. His words were stern. Uncompromising.

"Your husband must *come in* and sign, my dear woman. *Come in.*"

"Oh . . . but he is taking his nap, you see. And then we are to leave. I am to have the car packed and ready to go."

Filled with fatigue and frustration over the whole thing, the clerk took a deep, audible breath, ready with some final remonstrance. And I took my last shot.

"If I wake him, he will beat me," I said, lowering my eyes at the thought of it.

I can see the man now, no happier with me nor the turn of events but having little trouble envisioning the projected scenario. Finally, with eye-rolling reluctance he reached out stiffly to drop the car key in my hands.

I was out of the parking lot in seconds. I could hardly believe what I had done.

For a while as I drove, waves of guilt floated in and out of conscience like second-hand smoke. An ethical debacle! A travesty of gender-based discrimination to which I had submitted by *design*. But mainly I felt wildly victorious. I had taken a gamble consonant with survival Arab-style and I'd won. Anything less would have gotten me another bus ride and *changed not one thing* in car-rental policies. I had beaten an Arab man at his own game. And I luxuriated in the feat.

Arab women, I knew, were anything but weak; their strength simply found a different avenue of private and public expression. And I could be forgiven, surely, if as an anthropologist I was learning something of the strategy of poking holes in the extant power structure.

Amina, our all-purpose maid in Rabat, knew all about holes and control. Her primary strategy was to keep us all happy enough with her performance that she could enjoy all the privileges that might in any way attach to her role and never make us so unhappy that we would be punitive.

Since the apartment was so little occupied during the day, her work was not onerous. But Amina, fretful that this circumstance be interpreted as idleness—inviting some just censure—invented work. She would roll up the rugs, beat them, and hang them over the patio walls to air, then move on to stack our minimal inventory of furniture in a precarious tower while she cleaned around it, moving from room to room on her blasting course before undertaking a final, reverse track of wet-mopping.

It was quite impossible for me to get any work done with her in the house. Proposed modifications of her work pattern were unsettling and in any case ineffective. Her inexorable procession through the apartment shot up most of the morning. I took to scheduling interviews or going to the university until noon, at which time the house was marginally navigable.

I cooked, but Amina shopped for food. As she rightly communicated, I wouldn't recognize a bargain if I saw one and would be given the least-fresh produce. Dr. Girard pointed out what I had essentially known, that Amina got a cut from the merchants. That was standard. More of going-with-the-flow strategy of optimal living.

Another dividend Amina saw as legitimately hers, a rightful part of the job, was the identification of property with which she would decide I was essentially "burdened" and of which she might relieve me: a dress of Sarah's that was surely too small for her now, a blouse of mine missing two buttons that I hadn't worn since I'd been there, a dish I had failed to notice was chipped.

But she was often creatively helpful. She seemed genuinely to enjoy the children, and they looked forward to after-school activities with her. When my daughter showed interest in the hennaed hands and feet she'd seen on some women, Amina brought henna to the house and expertly drew designs on Sarah's hands, applying the little wet heaps of dye. Sarah learned how very long and patiently Arab women must wait if they were to be beautiful and the henna indeliblized. Beauty, anywhere in the world, had a price.

Amina was eager to fulfill your wishes, not to disappoint. All of which was fine, except for the maddening compulsion that made her presort our reactions as either favorable or potentially punitive—though we had never been even faintly harsh with her.

One day, for example, she arrived quite late for work. Normally it would not have mattered to me, but I had an appointment with a man who had carved out special time for me. Also the children had no school, and I was reluctant simply to leave them. At last Amina burst in.

"Thank goodness," I said. "I was beginning to think something had happened to you." I took a nervous look at my watch. Retrospectively I set up the whole fiasco that followed by interjecting that I *really* must not be late for an appointment. For Amina, the free translation was that she had placed me in what amounted to monumental jeopardy.

"I got hit by a bus," Amina announced without preamble. She was smiling.

"Oh, Amina!" I studied her in alarm. But there was not so much as a smudge on her.

At that point my son, Tom, walked in to welcome her. He was clearly glad to see her. "I was afraid you wouldn't come and tell us how to play the game."

"I fell off my bicycle," came from Amina.

My daughter was next in. "I knew you'd come. I told Mom you'd be here."

"My father beat me," Amina said, expressionless. Then she lifted her arms and put them loosely around my neck, the sleeves of her caftan touching my hair. "I'm sorry, my sister." And she went off with the children.

I suppose that Amina's father could have beaten her so that she raced away from the house on her bicycle and fell off it, whereupon she was hit by a bus. But the triad of casualties was implausible. Most telling was her embrace of me and the use of a kinship term, which automatically invited a special tolerance. She was seeking the empathy of a sister, not an employer. And all of this in the context of an environment that, if anything, had been an indulgent one.

But what I would came to understand was that this very advantage was what Amina had seen as terribly threatened. Three persons had been discomforted by her delay. Her explanation needed to be in keeping with the damage report. Whatever occurred . . . if she simply overslept, Amina needed to

translate the outcome into an incontestable act of heroic forti-
tude on her part.

As I left the apartment I could hear the children, still
quite upset about the tribulations heaped upon Amina, working their solace on her. Amina, once again her old self, had
already set about fixing them a fruit-flavored drink. The
kitchen had a half-dozen bottles of variously flavored syrups to
which soda water is added and stirred. Normally Amina simply
prepared whatever she chose, but today they were being told
they might *choose*. This indulgence, however trivial, was
clearly another gesture of contrition.

Wherever fieldwork has taken me, I have rarely found it
easy to move beyond the intellectualization of experience to
the somatization of it: to translate insight into the emotions,
into the physically guiding cues that, in tandem with intellect,
shape a people's world.

Over the months, Amina helped me approach that level
in Morocco . . . as did others: to identify with the flood of vulnerability, to rev up the body on cue with appropriate indignation, to "think" power when I wanted to send some small but
meaningful confirmation of privilege. "Acting" *is* living in the
Arab world. For, if topography does little to bond the inhabitants of the Arab world's regionally diverse peoples, a distinctive presentation of self (body and mind) does.

You are—or become—what people want you to be so as to
reap or retain respect. Hopefully cooperation. Minimally tolerance. Those with power protect or enlarge it. Those without
power try to project it or go with the flow—seeking a padded
protection within the system.

Learning to be Moroccan is learning the permanent mastery of putting your best foot forward. Not all that dissimilar
in some ways from many cultures of the world, but—criti-
cally—*shame-free*. Sania Hamady, herself an Arab, extends a
similar analysis generically to Arab temperament and character worldwide.[3] From childhood to maturity one pursues the

intricate art of presentation of a self that must constantly be recreated with amoeba-like fluidity.

Abdelwahad Radi, a British-educated Arab, who returned to Morocco to work and lecture, defined the stages of enculturation of the Moroccan child from birth to adolescence in what he saw as a pattern culminating in distrust of personal initiative and in unpreparedness for an adult role associated with independent, individualized responsibility.[4]

The Arab's very "social self" upsets Americans who, although rarely verbalizing it, anticipate a predictable consistency in social interactions, a fixed internal (not external) monitor of right and wrong. The Arab thrives on a "negotiable" self.

Shame and *guilt* are culturally entrenched formulas for survival. They produce (and are, in turn, a product of) distinct directions in formal and informal education, religious mandate, and legal systems. Both work. Both allow for self-esteem and national pride.

In the Arab world one accounts for one's actions to a viewing society; in ours, essentially, to that constant voice within. Neither world is privileged to enjoy a guileless membership. The concept of "sin" (that inner testament of wrongdoing) is not unknown to the Arab. But as one proverb has it: "A sin concealed is half-forgiven." Nor is there any inherent solace in a supportive group presence. "Distrust your enemies once, your friends a hundred times," runs another much-quoted saying. Yet the Moroccan is rarely a loner.

And there is a playful side to Moroccans. They like games—often at the expense of the foreigner—in which often they have nothing to gain or lose except the thrill of the match or the bewilderment they can call forth. Somehow the outlandish, the unlikely, or the absurd seem safer ground for untried social interaction.

Moroccans are, in fact, deeply religious, but their relation with God is relatively unfiltered by a hovering clergy. One's obligation are to Allah, direct and precise: praise, thanksgiving, prayer, prescribed good deeds and undertakings.

Whatever one's judgment of it, the Arab "self" has a lot going for it. Cross-culturally it has shown incontestable survival value and has spearheaded the spread of Islam. Life will go on, it promises, under a code of behavior more often endorsed than violated.

But despite my affection for Morocco and the lingering memory of its beauty, ours was a relationship flawed by an underlying cultural incompatibility. We were never meant for marriage.

Notes

1 Dorothy Gary and Lord Kinross, *Morocco,* 5 (New York: Viking Press, 1971).

2 Bernard Lewis, *The Arabs in History,* 9 (London: Hutchinson and Co., 1950).

3 Sania Hamady, *Temperament and Character of the Arabs* (New York: Twayne Publishers, 1960).

4 Abdelwahad Radi, "Processus de Socialisation de L'Enfant Marocain," in *Annales Marocaines de Sociologie* (Rabat: Institut de-Sociologie, 1969).

GENDER
AND
ETHNICITY

7

The Social Organization of the Service

A United States Military Base

Fieldwork in a controlled environment makes particular demands upon the cultural anthropologist. Undertaking it in the United States suggests the further need to develop what might be described as *hybrid vision*. Experience must be filtered through two interrelated cultural lens: that of the home "U.S." culture that we and our research subjects share, *plus* that of the "field arena," which is alien in the sense that those whose daily routines are lived out within it *must* respond to different learned and shared prescriptions for behavior (different from the "outside" world of which they are simultaneously a part). They live with a double cultural bind. The anthropologist must work within that bind.

One of my assignments in applied anthropology placed me on a United States military base that accommodated members of the U.S. Air Force, Army, and Navy. The research was exploratory in nature, limited in scope, and addressed sensitive issues. I was to identify and reconstruct particular themes that shape performance and expectations of women in the military. "Theme" here refers to patterns of shared attitudes underlying behavior as well as behavior itself. I would do a pilot report on women's assessment of their military careers. The year was 1988.

Women have become so integral a part of the armed services that it would be impossible to field a standing peacetime force of volunteers without them. Major General Jeanne Holm, who at the time of her retirement from the air force after 33 years of service had risen from truck driver to the highest-ranking woman ever to serve in the United States Armed Forces, saw women's impact on the military as "an unfinished revolution." "Revolution" in this context has reference to the influx of women under sanction of law into the previously all-male military; "unfinished," to her conviction that women's full incorporation within the ranks continues to constitute a major challenge for the armed services.

Attitudes on women's participation in the military have been documented as varying from beliefs that their presence enriches the services, to negative attitudes and fears of a diminished combat readiness because of them. Some researchers see the military as a male-generated model for optimal performance in war, essentially nonaccommodating of women without unwanted change.

Dispassionate literature is rare, despite an evident consensus that mutually respectful adaptation on the part of men and women is critical to effective growth in all branches of the service. There is agreement, also, that the military inevitably will change by virtue of women's presence. While the nature of that change has been variously considered, few venture an unequivocal description of the form it will take. Women in the military remain an enigma to many men. And G. B. Northcraft and J. Martin have shown how this lack of closure can act to aggravate negative expectations about *minority* women.[1]

In the terms spelled out in my initial assignment I was committed to an in-depth study of just twenty-four women, drawn from across the services, enlisted as well as officer personnel, and representing the views of African-Americans, Anglos, and Hispanics.

Eventually my work expanded. It would come to include: (1) the draft of a research instrument for potential use in a broader U.S. testing program, (2) an oral report for the base's senior staff on the completion of my assignment, and (3) a written report for the institute sponsoring the research. Any and all of my "views, opinions, and/or findings" would—appropriately—be clearly indicated as mine, as opposed to an official position of any branch of the services.

I entered a world in many ways as foreign as anything I'd known. Some of the hurdles were almost as fundamental as learning a new language. More accurately what was involved was the interpretation of a new symbolic system, a different information processing and dispersal network.

In this culture, uniforms are standard dress. Rank, a significant social variable, is visibly distinguishable (once you learn the code) and effects a salute system, forms of address, and power. Accolades of achievement, in forms of ribbons, braid, and metal, also convey crucial information.

Entry to the base is as controlled as that of a castle; guards are on duty. To get to my work I needed written validation on my person and visible validations on my car. Interpreting bugle calls (piped inside and outside buildings) that could bring pedestrian *and* motor traffic to a halt, developing the circumlocution involved in communicating my needs across an alien power structure, and understanding the relevance of commandeered space (anywhere): these were challenges not readily met. Nor was I aware I had been given a coveted private office in itself de facto evidence of the more than casual nature of my presence on the base.

I was introduced formally at one of the regular staff meetings, invited by various people for coffee, and quizzed with an amiable but predictable curiosity about what anthropologists generically *did*. Men and women were cordial. The base was large. Few people even knew I was around. But for those for whom I would be a daily or even intermittent presence, I warranted tracking. Eventually I would make friends, some of whom diplomatically steered me away from open craters during my initially myopic search for insight.

For a week or more after my arrival I moved about in the afterglow of a warm welcome by the base commander. Particularly buoying was his exhortation that I need only let the appropriate person know what my needs were, in the confidence those needs would receive attention.

Of course the free translation—had I known the language—was: don't make a move unless you tell someone what you're up to. He or she will then: (1) prescribe a safe course of action or (2) figure out a way to deflect or derail it. In fairness, the reader needs to know that this plan of action by the military was neither dramatic nor malicious. Making sense of a culture is a two-way street. What the anthropologist does, indeed what anthropology is all about—is as unnerving and portentous for the "native" as it is for the "intruder."

Effective anthropology involves respect and caution and the acquired practice of adapting one's thoughts, actions, and utterances to changing circumstances. The monitoring of all this exacts a diligent search for "connectedness." Actually, it's a little like putting together the ingredients of a recipe, the actual product of which unfortunately is not identified for you when you start working on it. If you do a fairly decent job, minimally you'll come up with something palatable and rewarding of the effort involved. Undue concern with the potential for failure produces nothing but garbage.

An often-used strategy (though not surefire) is to take one's cue from what others ("the natives") do. But the military was way ahead of me on strategy.

For my first couple of weeks on base, the officer designated to assist me inundated me with files. I was there for information. They would give it to me: a posture more literal than noncooperative. It proved useful. I was able to develop an employment history and profile for the modest but representative sample of women scientists, engineers, or technicians in whose military representation the sponsoring agency was particularly interested. What I lacked was generally forthcoming . . . and I was learning the art of fruitful request.

This empathetic climate cooled, however, when at the beginning of the third week I dropped the casual announcement that I now needed to *talk* to people.

By this time I had modified and redesigned the intensive interview questionnaire with which I had come to the assignment. It addressed various areas of government interest, including the women's lives prior to enlistment, their own review of enlistment history, and their plans and expectations for the future. Also, I changed the face page of the document from "Intensive Interview Questionnaire" to the more simple "Interview with Military Women"—a less invasive and challenging designation. I was learning the language of the base with its vocabulary of skilled communication.

I began my interviewing.

To my surprise women expressed no concern for anonymity. "I will tell it like it is," one enlisted woman said. And that verbal posture remained characteristic. Nevertheless, anonymity was in every case protected to the best of my ability. I developed an elaborate code, not only to their names, but to their location within the system.

I now moved more widely around what was an attractive base, beautifully planted with a military tidiness of greenery and flowers. One-on-one lengthy meetings were conducted within the privacy of a closed office. Most of the time I managed a low-keyed exchange. Often I could satisfy some of their curiosity about an anthropologist who apparently neither "dug" nor had lost her way en route to a more conventional site. I met with each of the twenty-four women three times in interviews that averaged three hours per session. Where women pursued lines of thought unanticipated within the formal framework of the interview they were encouraged to pursue them. Further probes—"Anything else?" "Could you elaborate on that?," "And then what happened?"—were incorporated when they seemed appropriate to the enlargement of the discussion.

I wound up with an avalanche of data.

An incontrovertible finding of the research was that these twenty-four subjects—African-American, Anglo, and Hispanic—are first and categorically "woman-focused" in their comments and concerns, and only secondarily invested in ethnically related issues. Black women, however, unanimously are sensitive to what they see as the double jeopardy of being black and female.

Across the services represented (air force, army, and navy) there is ethnic consensus that the military is democratically conceived. The women have great respect for the military. There is further accord that the criteria that determine progress within the system and assure its viability *are* appropriate. The services, they agree, can take justifiable pride in their antiracial and antiprejudicial posture on women.

However, they believe as well that the military is more democratic for men than for women, that the system as presently operating rewards men more equitably than women in their progression through it, and that the masculine genesis of the military continues to mitigate *full* sexual and racial equality. Women are aggressive and articulate in voicing these convictions and in their advocacy of change that would terminate what they view as disparity between what the system was designed to do and what it currently does—often to the detriment of women's advance within it.

Women see, in the words of a navy officer, "no great conspiracy. That's the way it has always been done. The service basically likes the status quo. And the status quo is male."

An enlisted air force veteran of twenty years insisted that "We are beginning to see change, but it hasn't touched male hearts and minds, and until it does or is made to, the real potential will just lie there—on the books." The air force sergeant who had responsibility in the hands-on repair and maintenance of aircraft voiced a widely shared sentiment: "It isn't so much opposition or even antagonism. Nothing you can come to grips with and say 'let's deal with it.' You adapt to the male stuff. If you complain or even find a way of doing it differently, you're being feminine."

Among Anglo, Hispanic, and African-Americans there is agreement that, as women, they must routinely work harder than men for the same rewards, pursue every advantage aggressively, and build around them a network of supportive women upon whom they rely in learning how to cope with the in-place male system. *Not* to do these things they regard as derelict, not only in order to improve women's image and because they believe this approach the best route to personal advancement, but because they want to be excellent at what they do.

"Take Helen. She's the only woman on that crew. She has to be more 'super' than a man on a 'super' job."

However, they believe the system is reasonable in that it provides for women (as for men) a designated route for rising in the military. "You advance by 'filling in all the squares': education, how you test, performance reports. They can get you there or you can run into trouble. Man or woman, when you get a bum rap there are resources. Racism or sexism doesn't stand the glare when you have hard evidence. The military does its best to stay clean, and you get a better shot here than on the outside."

In two contexts, however, the military is associated with impediments over which women have no control. Minority women regard them as influential in their underrepresentation in officer ranks and in the upper echelons of noncommissioned officers.

First and foremost is the de facto denial of women to combat-ready appointments when the absence of such experience makes them, in effect, ineligible for advancement to those ranks for which this experience is legitimately critical.

"On the one hand, the measure of our success as women is how we adapt in a man's world; on the other hand, there is a 'No Entry' sign on half of it," said an officer who was denied access to the kind of shipboard experience and training for which she sees herself fully qualified.

Women express their awareness of the political and humane debate in progress on women in combat and of the related ambiguities presently in place. What they can less willingly accept, in the words of one, is "the 'you can't-get-there-from-here' consequence in terms of promotion, travel, adventure, and power denied." They variously attach failure to effect change to the Congress, a diffident public, and those males who regard combat as "the point of entry to the last all-male club" and zealously protect it.

Secondly, women want a more empathetic view on the part of the military toward pregnancy and childbirth. This "burning issue" was addressed by Hispanic, African-American, and Anglo women despite the absence in my initial interview document of any question related to it.

Concerns are voiced on several levels. First and most frequent was the apparent conviction that present practices reflect a simple and unexamined extension of the priority of "masculinity" in the services. Second, women's sexuality is thought to be regarded by men as both a threat—"They think we came into the service to get pregnant or hunt husbands," and a burden—"Pregnancy is treated like some kind of crime against the system." The woman whose tour of duty took her out of the country within two months of the baby's birth insisted that this kind of separation was not rare. "When the baby arrives you are given thirty days. You can add to that two weeks of your own time. There needs to be a more realistic resolution."

Some women were vigorous in wanting it understood that "parenthood is not the exclusive domain of women." They do not see men inviting the same threat of stigma because they take on fatherhood while in the service: "Do they really think the only parents are women?" Another asked: "Why not leave for new fathers, particularly in households where both husband and wife are in the service?" Two such households were represented in this small sample.

In these issues of sex, femininity, and reproduction, women displayed least acceptance and a growing intolerance of what they regard as injustice or sexual harassment. Related jokes and gossip, often graphically repeated for my benefit, particularly offend them.

Finally, women want more opportunities for "mentoring": "First permanent duty station is where mentoring is needed. Special issues should be dealt with. Recruiters aren't doing it. Women need to talk with women—for their benefit and for the good of the services. Certainly women need to be prepared for the sexual pressures of military life. . . . As things stand, they are not."

Eventually I found myself grateful for the considerable time into which the interviews seemed to stretch. The looseness of much of our exchange provided an opportunity for women to signal priorities that would otherwise have escaped me. Relationships became friendlier ones.

Much of the consensus surprised me . . . though a larger sample may have proven more revealing. Yet, despite reservations about the quality of their careers, these women (with only three exceptions) would give a very favorable recommendation to military life if their daughters were to express interest in joining the service.

"If it were up to me," said one African-American enlisted woman, "I'd advise every individual in this country to serve some time in the military. There is unmatched potential for personal growth within it. A seasoning process. And once your wings develop . . . well, you can fly. And that's a good feeling. Something you can use for the rest of your life."

I had chosen not to record our sessions. A potentially accessible tape or disk might prove compromising. Instead I developed a technique of fast-paced writing, losing no more eye contact than I had to. Hugely helpful was my having learned shorthand, years before, during a waffling period about my own future. The downside was that, though adequate, my shorthand skills lacked the pristine accuracy with which I had initially committed the forms to memory. So, I needed faithfully to transcribe everything nightly. By the end of the months of research I was sleep deprived and weary of the long routine.

One Sunday afternoon I decided that I had been overplaying the self-sacrificial role. I was working in my office on the second floor of the base where, after some finagling, I'd gotten myself one of the coveted keys to an outside door. A lovely warm streak in the weather had turned the sky bright blue, and I simply flipped my notebook shut and took to the stairs.

The place was deserted. Or so I thought.

The bare wooden stairs creaked. And a man who had been standing with his back to the staircase turned, clearly surprised. It was the base commander, with whom I had not exchanged more than a few words since my arrival. With him was a boy about six, his son.

He remembered me.

"Well," he said, "I knew anthropologists were explorers . . . but I shouldn't think empty buildings have much appeal."

He was laughing. "Too nice a day. That's what my son tells me."

His hand was on his son's shoulder.

"Say hello to Dr. Anderson, Josh." We solemnly shook hands.

"Well, what do you think of the natives?" the commander asked. It was meant as a cordial overture.

"Friendly," I said.

"Good, good. . . . Well, I won't keep you." But in the few seconds it took me to smile a good-bye to Josh, he went on: "Look, I hope you'll come back. Another time. Think about talking to the men. Interview the men next time. I would certainly go along with that."

Return to the base? *Not a bad idea*, I thought, meeting the commander's eyes. The men were certainly entitled to equal time and the delineation of their own "themes" of the military. But it was doubtful I'd be coming back.

The commander, however, had not finished.

"I know you were thrown a few curves," he said. "I could have made things easier."

It was sweet to hear. But I was honest when I told him I would be leaving with no resentment and a great deal of satisfaction.

"Well . . . keep in touch. You may change your mind. Phone . . . Phone *me*."

There was no way I could suppress my laugh.

"This is Anderson. Pass me through to the commander. . . Codeword . . ." I had him laughing "I'll need a codeword, won't I, commander?"

The commander looked down at the now restless Joshua.

"Can you think of a good codeword for Dr. Anderson, Josh?"

There was the barest of pauses from the apparently hungry as well as impatient Joshua.

"Alphabet soup," Joshua said. "Alphabet soup would be good."

I agreed.

Alphabet soup said it all.

Note

[1] G. B. Northcraft and J. Martin, "Double Jeopardy," in *Sex Role Stereotyping and Affirmative Action Policy,* ed. G. A. Gutek (Los Angeles: Institute of Industrial Relations, University of California, 1982).

ACHIEVING GROUP IDENTITY

8

The Ordering of Human Relationships

A Hot Bath and a Cup of Tea in Japan

Over the years I have become stringent about taking the time to record my first impressions of a country or a field situation. These are valuable but fragile data—a kind of cultural-entry baseline.

Walking about with a notebook is awkward, but at the end of the day or during a lunch break or on a bus or train it's a smart thing to do. Back home again these observations evoke the "skin" of a culture, with insights different from the subsequent "dissection" that comes with more topical "insider" interviews. The latter give critical flesh to the anthropologist's research, bulk to the data. They are the stuff of fieldwork. But I have never sold first impressions short . . . even if I have to revise hasty conclusions reached from them.

In Japan, from the first days, something about the very physicality of the country's island status spoke to *containment:* a containment that translates into a definition of space very different from the limitless sweep of American plains where openness goes on seemingly forever.

Japan suggests too a different equation between person and object. Small tea cups; no giant mugs. Slender chopsticks that make picking up grains of rice an art form . . . a very different exercise from spearing a Texas-size steak with a serrated knife and a reasonably weighted fork.

As cultures Japan and the United States seem to invite different scales of energy. Smaller, tidier people generally, the Japanese traveled in smaller cars or in trains whose ceiling was sometimes a challenge for the "exceptionally" tall. I was prepared for and familiar with the Japanese physiognomy, but I remember the awe that seized me when I looked from the back row of a theater to the stage and realized for the first time that *everyone*'s hair was black except for the few gray-haired ones that stood out as flamboyantly as a carrot-redhead might in the United States.

Stylistically Japan was lopsided. In some of the least expected places there was a display of elegance side-by-side with almost abusive disregard: the dauntingly formalized greetings and good-byes, bodies scrupulously postured in multiple bows in synchronized timing, while right beside these people—in a railroad station—uniformed employees were literally pushing stray arms and legs of commuters into mobbed cars.

My breath caught at the beauty of small backyard ponds and of rural lakes and mountains that, in the purity of dusk, were amazingly like what I had previously thought of as contrived woodcuts and screens; yet, in areas of Tokyo, the pollution level caught one's breath in a different way and the muted color of the sky had a very different genesis.

For the outsider, life in Japan is both disarming and disturbing. For the field anthropologist, cultural participation means learning to function by responding to ground rules of *incorporation* and *distancing*. It means recognizing the signals of: (1) welcomed passage or (2) the do-not-disturb sign. This is not easy.

In the Japanese mind there is something eternally non-transferable about the benefits that accrue from having been born Japanese. This includes a shared view of the proper ordering of human relationships as well as attributes of the natural world. Essentially, those individuals who are not Japanese are cultural aliens. Benevolent sometimes but feeble learners . . . as I was.

Once the considerable duration of my visit became apparent, I needed to apply for an Alien Card. Failure to renew the card promptly at designated periods made necessary not only paperwork, a fine, and an agency visit but also a letter of apology (for abusing a social courtesy).

The Japanese have attracted much anthropological interest in the area of social organization. And not surprisingly. As I would gradually learn, person-to-person or nation-to-nation, Japan has a hallowed recipe for virtually every interaction. Basically, Japanese life is a dyad: a matter of laboring the desired into precious predictability and removing or ignoring the rest. This duality applies to dimensions of the natural as well as the social world. That this compromise is not readily achieved is attested by the centuries the Japanese have spent refining the challenge involved, and encoding for the common good those formula that proved useful. "Useful" here refers to patterns of behavior which, if scrupulously duplicated, will sustain or advance the desired social equation. In interactions with society, as with nature, the product should be a harmonious one. Indeed Japan's natural, embracing, geographic world is the cradle within which all harmony is either advanced or compromised.

Prescriptions for action, I began to realize, are most evident in Japanese art forms . . . in themselves much favored as models of restraint. For the Japanese, social organization in a sense imitates art. Put differently, *culture itself is an art form.*

The "National Treasures" recognized yearly by the emperor are *people*, not objects.

The genesis of this togetherness of social and artistic expression gradually became more fathomable. From the meticulous writing style, to the ordained movements of greeting and farewell, to the presentation of food: the "aura" of communication is as vital as the message. Aura *becomes* message. The social code (invisible) is as effectively communicated to the young Japanese student as the action code (visible). Both derive from tried and true formulas variously embraced and predictably indulged.

My own interest in things Japanese began early. . . from the time of my childhood friendship in the United States with a Japanese girl. Her father had the neighborhood tailoring shop. Toyoko and I were in and out of each other's houses after school.

My father, I remember, had trouble pronouncing her name and affectionately dubbed her "Tapioca"—a nickname that made her laugh but whose use today might well propel him into court.

I loved their small apartment above the shop, the spare furnishings, the few pieces of art so effectively placed, the several kimonos. During World War II she and her family were carted off to a detention camp. I never learned what happened to them.

The friendship spawned no fluency in Japanese. But something remained. The remembered rhythm of exchanges between her father and mother. The "differentness" of the many things that had given stability and animation to our separate worlds. And years later when the opportunity arose to spend serious time in Japan I leaped at it. I had made one previous visit en route to a field site elsewhere, long enough to rekindle interest in the Japanese way of life.

Though I'm not sure I could have framed my thinking in quite that way at the time, I had retained the conviction that Japanese culture did an exceptional job of paralleling aesthetic with social appreciation *across generations*. And the more I worked in aging research, the more convinced I became that something in these emphases might prove a therapeutic resource in later life.

This idea was too amorphous a basis for serious financial support, but during a sabbatical year, I got myself funded on a modest combination research/lecture grant that included housing at our "sister university" in Japan. When I arrived, I learned that additionally, from time to time, I would join a cadre of psychologists and psychiatrists in Osaka who had an interest in aging adaptation. For me it was a magical and privileged mix.

As a visitor to their country, armed with these critical social connections, I experienced insight into the dynamics of much of Japanese life that would otherwise have eluded me. My Japanese-anchored credentials opened doors, illuminating codes of conduct and life styles in homes and offices . . . and sometimes beyond.

The men (with whom I was most in professional contact) spoke English with various levels of competence. Two of the professors and one M.D. had done graduate-level study in the United States. But for broader, hands-on fieldwork I knew I could not be mute in Japanese. And in anticipation of that problem, the terms of my grant had subsumed the intensive study of Japanese prior to leaving the United States at a language institute whose much-publicized credentials included World War II training of intelligence officers. My competence, let me hasten to say, was never to approximate the level they achieved. Indeed, after my brief six weeks of study no right-minded government would have chosen overclose identification with me.

Nevertheless training was merciless: six hours per day of one-on-one contact with three separate language coaches. I also had homework on the fundamentals of *hiragana* and *katakana* language scripts. Taking on the really critical ideograms was never a consideration; Japanese students spend years mastering the thousands of them.

Two days after completion of the program I was put on a plane, far from fluent but ten pounds lighter.

Language expressiveness is important to all Japanese. The "art" of indirection is as critical to the language of business and general socialization as it is to the highly distinctive forms of Japanese poetry and theater. The American "I-tell-it-like-it-is" approach to social exchange will find you left in an empty room in Japan. One of the most telling comments on the country was later voiced by a Japanese colleague, citing an unidentified treatise that reminded the reader there are "16 ways to say *No* in Japanese." He delighted in pointing out to me that "No" is not one of them.

My stumbling through half-completed sentences was rarely disturbing. They got the drift. If anything it aroused in my concerned listeners the empathetic need to let me know they followed my thoughts . . . even when I could not.

In this sustained kindness, not only were they being socially supportive, but (in further testimony of the intractable roots of Japanese togetherness) it was not expected that an outsider could really master the Japanese language. Facing this same corporatively generated view of language, my bilingual Japanese-born neighbor in the university's "traditional-housing" quarter failed miserably in convincing anyone that his adopted, American-born (but ethnically Japanese) daughter could not speak Japanese. Raised in the United States, where her father had been university-affiliated for two decades, the young woman's command of Japanese could not have exceeded one hundred laboriously acquired words. At seventeen it was her first visit. Nevertheless, Japanese consensus in effect was that—with all those genes working—she could speak vastly better Japanese if she just let herself go. Let it all out. The right impetus was somehow lacking.

On the other hand, I met two expatriated Americans and one Frenchman who, from whatever scenario of necessity or choice, spoke apparently flawless Japanese. All expressed the often-met Japanese awe of their accomplishment—as though, in the words of one: "I had overcome some physiological or genetic impairment." The Japanese are not unkind in this. They are incredulous.

Like the French, of whom they often reminded me, the Japanese thrive in ordered universes with prescriptions for any interaction. Indeed few treatises on Japanese culture are without according great historical depth to the evolution of commitment to discipline. The expected outcome is concrete achievement, a diversity of skills, and if not perfection—something very close to it.

Robert Frager narrates the story of a seventeenth-century *samurai* whose magnificent sword attracted the attention of three seedy and predatory onlookers as he dines in a small country inn. He appeared an easy target, dullishly unbothered by four flies hovering about his plate: "He seemed to take no notice and their remarks became ruder and more pointed. The swordsman merely raised his chopsticks. In four quick snips, he effortlessly caught the four flies on the wing. As he slowly laid down the chopsticks, the three *ronin* left the room."[1]

What is then revealed to us is that the man was Musashi, one of Japan's greatest swordsman and famous as well as philosopher, artist, and calligrapher. What Frager wants us to understand in the Musashi tale (even if, as he suggests, apocryphal) is that "pocketed" technical excellence or efficiency, however prized, is not the ultimate goal of training. Rather, discipline becomes a force that reshapes one mentally as well as physically. In the case of Musashi, art and swordsmanship as it were nourished one another in a palette of achievements. And that "powerhouse" was what the three men instantly recognized in Musashi.

But the Japanese, for all their readiness, are not fond of confrontation, avoid it if they reasonably can, and as a culture have devised ways to imbue the ordinary with distinctive social grace.

Consider a hot bath or a cup of tea. In Japan both have been culturally reshaped from vehicles for: (1) restoration to cleanliness or, (2) the alleviation of thirst—to a pool party and a sacrament, respectively. In unburdening participants *collectively* from real or potential stress, each in its own way offers the rewards that flow from an achieved harmony.

The tea ceremony does it with a tight script. The bath, with an approved abandon: it has been called the grand passion of the Japanese people.[2]

There is something in the psyche of most Americans that would be seriously strained by the experience of walking buck-naked into the company of strangers. The only worse scenario would be doing it with *friends*—similarly unattired.

Ofuro is the generic name given to the Japanese bath. The communal (sometimes sex-segregated) bath is widely found in various forms. My initial experience with "the bath" was in the Hakone mountains on the fringe of Mount Fuji. The area is one of exquisite vistas. Some of the local inns have outdoor baths within gardens that achieve the look of a wooded grove, fortuitously stumbled upon, and sparely embellished with large well-spaced, elegantly misshapened stones. I had arranged to arrive at one such inn in advance of my university commitment, seeking relaxation after a hectic exit from the United States.

Having expressed to a solicitous maid my desire for a bath before dinner, I found myself under her watchful supervision. She twice sent me back to my tatami-floored room. Once because I had made the wrong choice from two kimonos provided and the second time because I had overlapped the kimono inappropriately before encasing my waist with the wrong *obi* or sash. The creative product, I was solemnly informed, is appropriate only for corpses.

She guided me across the inn's several terraces. A full moon was already visible. And it was a second or two before I realized that I was not staring at its reflection on some shiny rooftop, but at gleaming water, across whose extensive surface was an arched walkway, like the handle on some giant basket and over which I was guided and made to surrender my kimono to an attendant who was unamused by my reluctance to let go of it for want of anything with which to cover my naked body. She guided me through the critical brief wash and rinse after which I was encouraged to slip into water that was probably not quite hot enough to poach an egg.

I suppose that on a bleak December night, when thin-walled housing makes its limitations felt, opulent levels of heat would have greater appeal than the mid-July experience had for me. As the only Westerner in the place, I attracted attention but, with the offhanded Japanese acceptance of nudity, no one's interest was keen. Men and women, whole families, soaked and bobbed about in sublime contentment.

"It is good," one woman told me, in answer to my probing about the seduction of scalding water, "to feel the heat, like maybe sometimes anger, and then in a little while go out in the cooler air. Always the air is cooler. Even in summer the bath is hotter. You relax. Everybody together. No problems . . . problems *melt*."

I am not sure how far the analogy can be pushed but, over the months, I would find myself routinely surprised by the frequency with which social symbolism was so readily transposed into a words-and-body art form.

Eventually I would learn as well that, on occasion "the bath" can serve very calculated social needs. The bath is a social "leveler." Nudity is rankless.

An example comes to mind. In the course of my academic year at our Japanese "sister university," I managed to negotiate a field site for one of my Texas-based graduate students, an Okinawa-born woman of Japanese parentage who was fluent in Japanese. She needed a village within which to carry out a study of the status of traditional medical systems.

Placement was a product of the volunteered intervention of an administrator within what was now my "Japanese Alma Mater." He contacted a former classmate—from his own university days twenty years before. The man's sizable farm was well located, and the student would have the great advantage of vicarious identification with the community. She would be saved the trial of wandering about for a suitable location. *And* her eventual productivity and scientific recognition would reflect on both American and Japanese universities . . . further advancing the bonds of sisterhood.

As with all worthwhile undertakings in Japan, the details took some perking time, so that I was out of the country before I could properly express my appreciation to everyone involved. But when I got home I wrote several letters and sent off a couple of gifts as a small gesture of appreciation. Gifts are big in Japan. Gifts and their proper packaging.

Predictably, everything went according to plan. Not only did my student get her site, but she got a *home* with the gracious farm family. The village proved ideal, and she had status in it.

Six months later I was again briefly in Japan, en route elsewhere. By now inarguably a certified member of the fictive-kinship network[3] of the university community, I was met at the airport and escorted to my lodging. The next day I made the trip to the fairly distant area within which my student-colleague had now been working for several months.

My taking off by train *on my own* into an area of Japan unfamiliar to me was something I would have to answer for when I got back. I knew that. Assurance would have to be forthcoming that this infraction of reasonable social policy was of *my* genesis—not a reflection upon a host community that should minimally have arranged my travel. Indeed, one of the downsides of Japanese "togetherness" for those not rooted in the dynamics of its enculturation is facing the not-uncommon distrust of independent action—given a "group" alternative. Even worse is evidence that one is happier undertaking it.

But I *was* expected by the village family. The well-traveled household head marketed agricultural products beyond Japan and spoke some English. He and his wife made me welcome. My student brought me up to date on her impressive progress and guided me around the community within which she now stood as a kind of "stepdaughter" of her "substitute family"—a position that affected terms of address. My hosts insisted we all celebrate our togetherness with dinner out.

The evening would prove memorable. I assumed we'd eat somewhere within the village, but instead we drove for miles through exquisite country landscapes before pulling up to a small inn.

The Japanese, I knew, are markedly respectful of teachers. And I was perhaps overly sensitive to my role as "sensei" (frequently used as an honorific term of reference or address) and to whatever presentation of self should attach to minimally responsible image making. Despite a limited field wardrobe, I had been careful to dress the part.

The last thing I was prepared for was the inn's "disrobing rooms" and the "onsen" or spa large enough to hold the nude four of us and within which we luxuriated in water steamy enough to turn my hair to limp strings. Any social strictures attaching to student–teacher–host complications melted happily away—*as planned*. Later we dined in kimonos, relaxed and garrulous. I barely made the last Osaka-bound train . . . after pledges for reunion.

It is rare to find oneself in a Japanese house for more than ten minutes without being offered tea. But *Chanoyu* is not your run-of-the mill cup of tea. *Chanoyu*, literally hot water for tea, is variously written of as a ceremony, a rite, even a sacrament.

If the Japanese bath can be thought of as contributing to a more relaxed, restructured "now," the tea ceremony must be understood as going well beyond that modest goal. It speaks to a different equation with harmony and togetherness. Kikou Yamata tells us that:

> This purely spiritual ceremony of aesthetic enjoyment confers on the Japanese the worship of simplicity, together with respect for true beauty and sympathy with Nature. It develops self-control, a

noble attitude, and the gift for essential gestures. The feeling of passing time links the participants with eternity.[4]

Classically three or more hours long, the tea ceremony clearly sends a grander message than a soak in the pool.

I participated in four classical tea ceremonies. The most memorable of these complex dramas was at a training center in Kyoto. The ceremony was at the hands of one of the *grand masters*, men whose special claims to excellence are as appreciated as those of any master artist or swordsman, whom they are thought to match in elegance and control. For grand masters the classic rites are immutable.

The roots of the tea ceremony are most often linked to the fifteenth-century court of a *shogun* in Kyoto. However, green tea (thought to have medicinal value), reduced to a powder and beaten frothy, was appreciated even earlier by Buddhist monks who used it for the enhancement of *meditation*—or minimally to stay awake during the long hours committed to meditation. Communal bowls of tea were said to have been consumed before Buddhist images.

In any case, the shift from monastery to court occurred as the tea ceremony became an instrument for *mediation* between feudal adversaries. The architecture of the classic tea house (with a narrow entrance unsuitable to the bearing of swords), the structural imagery of the ceremony, even its lengthy time frame were designed to take participants beyond a fixed and troubled "now" into the peace of "timelessness" and a redrawing of the future.

Today the ideal setting for the centuries-old ceremony remains as rustic as resources allow, with a surrounding garden or minimally some vista of rocks, trees, or water. Guests are no longer expected to negotiate a narrow entrance on hands and knees, but the initial impact should foster the kind of humility that made its removal from the grandeur of a palace reception room a necessity. Inside and outside, a minimalist beauty suggests its own rewards; ostentation has no place in the accoutrements of service or interaction.

The long, simple, but aesthetically brilliant rules governing preparation of the tea and the etiquette of its consumption are designed to defuse aggressive intent and passion.

After my first tea ceremony, I was not only "defused" but, I feared, incapable of *standing*. At some point I had gone beyond "peace" to numbness, to excruciating pain from legs folded unrelievedly into alien positions under my body—Japanese fashion. Later I would master the art of sliding, by imperceptible inches from hip to hip, shifting periodically the pressure on my leg muscles.

Jack Seward tells an endearing account of his first tea ceremony.[5] As the frothy, bitter mixture was offered to the five guests and the cup passed (with prescribed sipping, bowl-turning, bowl-wiping routines) from one to the next, to be finished by the last, Seward made a surprising discovery. Later, when they were alone, he pointed out to his host that the tea cup was cracked, thinking he did not know. The misshapened, crudely colored tea cup, his host explained "had been made that way two hundred years before and was extremely valuable." The forms of nature, he went on to point out, are always imperfect and asymmetrical. The tea ceremony, held as it is in the garden and at appropriate seasons of the year is a reflection of nature.

Over two million Japanese are said to be devotees of the rite in one form or another.

The least engaging is an abbreviated forty-minute version designed by some hotels for the entertainment of time-limited tourists.

It is tempting to see in the Japanese "bath" or tea ceremony an open door to an easy comprehension of Japanese social organization or Japanese character. But, advisedly, anthropologists are trained to be cautious in reporting standards of behavior, their genesis, and expression. Outer trappings of behavior can be too readily accepted as the inviolable script of life. Anywhere in the world, what lies beyond the purview of hovering audiences must also be uncovered.

And toward this goal protracted participant observation is critical. Whether or not we are able eventually to identify with the people we study, to comprehend the range within which a person conforms to cultural codes or bends them or manages to skirt them or innovate: in these efforts our relative success always is hard to gauge.

Recent literature plays with the role that the anthropologist's own myopia and general intellectual and emotional baggage contributes to reporting. Fair enough. But most of us are very aware that, in both the observation and translation of behavior, full "purity" of effort (whatever that means) is implausible.

Despite, or perhaps because of, a "thick" social conscience, the Japanese show themselves to be remarkably introspective. Books by Japanese about Japanese durably are bestsellers. In the face of dramatic post–World War II reverberations, most express concern but confidence about the future. However, tinkering for tinkering's sake with the established order of things does not have the cultural appeal in Japan that it enjoys in the United States.

I once asked a Japanese friend about change and the future of Japanese culture.

"Japan has one time zone," was his reply.

I thought he had misunderstood me.

But he shook his head. "One time zone, one race, ten thousand years." He gave me a sly smile. "What are you going to change about that?"

Notes

[1] Robert Frager, "The Psychology of the Samurai," *Psychology Today* 2, 8, (1969) 48–49.

[2] Jack Seward, "The Japanese," in *Reader's Digest Condensed Books*, ed. John T. Beaudoin (Pleasantville, NY: 1972), 2:317.

[3] "Fictive kinship": any of various arrangements through which previously related or unrelated persons establish special interactions and take on obligations similar to those of particular kin, notably by adoption, godparenthood, and institutionalized friendship.

[4] Kikou Yamata, "The Tea Ceremony," in *Japan*, ed. Dore Ogrizek (London: McGraw-Hill Book Company, 1957), 307.

[5] Jack Seward, "The Japanese," in *Reader's Digest Condensed Books*, ed. John T. Beaudoin (Pleasantville, NY: 1972), 2:306.

ART AND ANTHROPOLOGY

9

All the World Sings
Jeannette MacDonald Is Alive and Well in Corsica

In the field, anthropologists develop various scenarios or styles of working. The nature of the research may well prioritize some approaches over others, but the selectivity with which anthropologists pick their way through the minefield of problems varies.

There are always problems. The bulk of these derive from our inherently disadvantageous position vis-à-vis the local community. Even when engaged in work at the invitation of national or international agencies, we must turn for answers to men and women who rarely have a clue as to why we are underfoot, or what we do.

Seldom are they enchanted with our presence. In the field we all too often translate as: (1) invasive, (2) unfathom-

141

able, (3) given to seemingly purposeless ways, and (4) often, accurately enough, less knowledgeable than children about the most fundamental dimensions of local life.

A recurrent nightmare is of some banal encounter that suddenly goes awry, making it impossible to complete one's work in a creditable way. A worst-case scenario is that of being thrown out of the community (an apprehension reinforced from graduate student days by stories of veterans of these experiences).

Admittedly the course of wisdom in fieldwork is to begin with the least confounding, least threatening overture to whatever population holds one's research potential in its collective hands. Chronic time constraints built into most applied assignments make this low-gear approach a luxury; but, even here, discretion and the advantage of goodwill are worth the time involved.

"Safe" areas of focus, however, are unpredictable. A seemingly simple question can evoke amusement in India, derision in France, and permanent government scrutiny in Russia or China. But over the years I have found that an expressed interest in a people's art forms is generally well received. A humanizing link attaches to the anthropologist's curiosity and sometimes provides a plausible opening to more sensitive issues.

I know of no culture without songs. Ethnomusicologists have signaled the considerable relevance of songs which, even when borrowed, are shaped locally to shared emotional experiences and expectations.[1]

The most cautious of men and women unwind and make sure you do not go away unappreciative of their musical heritage. On two occasions, however, the dividends of my interest proved more complex than I anticipated, though not without gained insight and a windfall of privilege whether I wanted it or not.

The place was the Mediterranean island of Corsica, south of Italy and north of Sardinia. There, in a remote mountain community I stumbled on a mystery involving the words and music of a local hymn; later, in the capital city of Ajaccio, I found myself elevated to the position of goodwill ambassador for the much-appreciated talents of an American singer, and all doors were opened to me.

I arrived in Corsica in 1969 on a flight from London, after a mind-numbing five-day international conference. It was summer. I had no serious commitments to bring me home, and I wanted to check out Corsica for possible fieldwork. "Island culture" continued to intrigue me. I had been curious about Corsica from the time a fellow student told me stories about it. But my trip could not have been more badly timed.

"You will sleep in the streets!" a horrified hotel manager told me when I arrived reservationless in Bastia on Corsica's northeastern coast.

Corsica was celebrating the 200th anniversary of the birth of Napoleon, the island's all-time national hero, born in Ajaccio one year after Corsica wrested political control from Italy (from the Genoese actually), to become a French possession.

"We have been booked for weeks and weeks," the manager went on. "So has every hotel on the island."

Local travel agencies were equally tragic. Nor was there much prospect of my scheduling a return flight. I could not rent a car. The woman at the rental agency was more awed than pitying.

"All the same, I think it was a very brave thing to do. Just to see our island, just to join in our celebration." She studied my face, which apparently looked sufficiently stricken for her to reach out and put a consoling hand upon my arm. "Just a moment . . . I have an idea."

She disappeared for about ten minutes, during which I decided that the evident strategy was not to be overly ready to disclose my actual ignorance of the nature of the celebration I had so courageously undertaken to share.

She returned, visibly animated, and beckoned me to the end of the counter. When she spoke her voice was low.

"I can get you to Corte."

"Corte?"

"Corte. About fifty miles from here. An eagle's nest. Once our capital. High, high in the mountains. The focal point of Corsica, symbol of resistance. And," her shoulders straightening perceptibly, "where there is located the house from which Laetitia Bonaparte, with Napoleon in her womb, set forth with her husband, Charles Bonaparte, walking along the goat tracks and on to Ajaccio, where Napoleon was born."

I could think of nothing to say. My silence seemed to please her.

"We have a car that must be returned to the rental agency in Corte, and I can arrange for you to take it there." She produced a file and took from it several papers. "As of noon today the woman for whom it was booked is overdue."

The narrative of my projected salvation went on.

"In Corte there is a priest, *my cousin*, who has a summer retreat house for men who come for a week of contemplation and prayer. There is always an extra bed. I will phone him you are coming."

"I—I don't know how to thank you."

She raised her hand.

"You will not thank me if you are stranded there."

Nevertheless, I was going to Corte. Who could resist? And I told her so, still bubbling with gratitude. One crisis at a time, I have learned, is good field policy. But she was ahead of me.

"My *sister's godfather* drives the bus that makes the trip from Corte to the southern tip of the island—the city of Bonifacio. And, if you wish, once you are in Corte you can find the bus schedule and I will give you a note to him . . . but afterward . . . from Bonifacio . . ." Her voice faltered and her hand went out, palm up, in a Corsican lap-of-the-Gods projection of my subsequent destiny.

But I had stopped worrying. I was on a roll. Corte and Bonifacio!

Once I had left the sleek eastern coastal rim, the mountainous interior doubled my projected driving time. As I climbed, a sense of eerie isolation drifted in and out of consciousness as the road found and then abandoned unrelieved stretches of *maquis*. Maquis is the dense plant growth that gave its name to the World War II resistance fighters who elusively escaped in and out of its bushes to hammer Nazi invasion attempts. The pleasing scents of lavender and of rosemary alert one to massive pockets of it.

Within Corte, dusk was wrapping itself around the tilted city before I managed directions to the church of Father Zerga—"Zerga," one of the many names linguistically echoing Italian "Genoese" influence on the indigenous Corsican language. But I was easily understood in French, the language of most education and commerce.

Father Zerga was pastor/director of a lean but elegant "abbey" enclosing a retreat house and church, which he immediately showed me: a gem of stained-glass windows, stations of the cross in mellow painted wood, and a marble altar with inlays of silver and gold. The whole was little larger than a chapel. I would be accommodated in a tiny, private room with bed, nightstand, a shelf of drawers, a vase of field flowers, and a window that overlooked the world! The price was whatever I chose to give.

I wanted to know more about Corte and this place. The day was Saturday and I asked if I might join the other guests at Mass on Sunday. Perhaps I ventured, there was a choir.

"A High Mass is sung at ten o'clock," he told me.

"A Latin mass?"

"Oh, yes." He looked at me, quite aware I was fishing for something. And I decided to share with him my interest in learning something about *Corsican* music. I was wondering if there might be an opportunity somewhere in Corte to hear local Corsican *songs*.

"Ah-h-h." He nodded his head. "But it is the old women who sing them best, and yes, they sing many. Many. Lullabies . . . love songs. But as for the hymns . . ."

I should have to come to 6:00 A.M. mass when I would hear the songs that have been sung every Sunday for decades. I was most welcome, as I would be for breakfast after if I chose.

At 6:00 A.M. the sky was still struggling toward dawn. The only light in the chapel was from three dim electric globes and the heavy altar candles. But banks of small yellow ones had begun to contribute to the glow as women (there were no men) set them to flame with waxed wands.

Father Zerga emerged from the sacristy with a young altar boy with still-damp hair. By now thirty or forty women filled the rows. They rose as he walked to the front of the altar, each of them poised above a straw kneeler. Indistinguishable from one another, in dark shawls, only their movements separated the women's forms from the dark interior of the chapel.

Father Zerga moved up the several steps of the altar and in a low voice read the Introit. I had located myself dead-center in one of the several vacant rows behind the presumably regular congregation of dawn mass.

Except during the Credo, which Father Zerga read in a voice that carried, the women sang. It was the third hymn, begun as the altar boy lifted and shook the small Communion bell, that got my rapt attention.

I could scarcely believe my ears as I strained to make some sense of the muted words. But there was no mistaking the melody, virtually every note of it. What was incomprehensible was how a secular hundred-year old American song, a stage favorite, had reached this remote, hill-steeped Corsican community. And in this religious transformation!

When Mass was over and the women funneled past me or walked forward to light yet another candle, I barely resisted following Father Zerga into the sacristy where he would remove his chasuble and in a few minutes, in all likelihood, head for the dining room.

I was there, waiting, when he walked in with a gracious smile, an arm lifted in welcome.

"You shall have some fine local bread, eggs and coffee strong enough to wake you—something I suspect we could both use." He led me to what was evidently his table with a cloth napkin folded into a silver band and another napkin, squared and crisp, marking my place.

I contained myself until there was food in front of us and Father Zerga, head lowered, whispered a swift grace. Someone filled my cup with steaming coffee.

"Father," I launched out, "I couldn't believe my ears."

"Really?" He looked pleased but puzzled at my apparent zeal.

"You don't understand . . . The music. That Communion song. That was pure Stephen Foster! Tempo slower, a few oddly repeated passages. But Stephen Foster? Here?"

"Stephen Foster?" Father was curious but undismayed as he offered me a thick slice of bread. I put it on my plate and he took one himself, posed his fork over his eggs, and met my eyes again inquiringly.

"Swanee River" . . . those women were singing "Swanee River"[2] with an ardor that would not have been out of place in Georgia. An American classic . . . an all-time break-your-heart folk song of the American South. A vocal testimony to homeland fidelity."

I was hopelessly carried away.

"Just listen," I went on struggling for the precise lyrics: "'Way down upon the Swanee River . . . far, far away.'" I was singing. "'That's where my heart is yearning e-v-e-r. That's where the old folks stay. All the world is dark and dreary, everywhere I r-o-a-m!'" And I ran out of lyrics.

I was now very nearly on my feet, arms extended to the table's edge. And I had Father Zerga's full attention. The only fortunate circumstance was that the dining room was otherwise empty—except for the hypnotized young waiter framed in the doorway, a platter of fruit in his hands.

I slipped back into my chair.

Father Zerga studied me briefly and then took a long swallow of coffee. "Let me see if I understand this," he said at last.

And I realized for the first time that I had sung, wretchedly, of course, and apparently incomprehensibly, in *English*. But how does one translate "Swanee River" into French . . . or *Corsican*? Which was precisely my question.

"Our communion song is known in the United States. Is that what you are telling me?"

"Your 'communion song' has been known in the United States since . . ." Here I struggled for a date. When did Stephen Foster live? "It has been sung in the United States for at least a century." My assessment was rapid, hazy, but, I knew, not far off.

Yet even as I spoke, I found in myself something quite uncommendable, bizarrely defensive, as though I were willfully uprooting some seedy Corsican borrowing, a vitiation of what was now as patently part of Corsican heritage as the mountains and maquis were part of the Corsican landscape.

Father Zerga broke the silence.

"Ah-h-h, I see where you are going . . . very interesting."

I couldn't leave it alone.

"What I am wondering, Father," I persisted, "is how Stephen Foster's music got from the showboats of the United States to the chapels of Corsica?" Then I gave him my most empathetic smile.

I knew the song that had been sung in his chapel was old, went innocently back a long way, even in the memories of the aged shawl-clad women who apparently sustained it. That much he had shared with me. Surely he could now speculate as to the route of cultural borrowing. Offer some clue as to the how of the music's incredible journey. Brought home perhaps by a returning emigrant? A chance find in some music library? Simply heard somewhere?

The server reappeared and filled our cups. Father Zerga reached out to put some berries on his plate from a bountiful fruit platter.

"I was wondering," he said at last in his still amiable and careful French, "if another explanation might not have occurred to you."

"Father?"

"We are celebrating, you know, the 200th anniversary of the birth of Napoleon."

I nodded. *Napoleon?*

"The name of that hymn, in Corsican, translates as 'Hymn of Thanksgiving for God and Country' and is particularly popular in our churches at the moment, inasmuch as it is associated with the 1769 liberation of Corsica, at which time the words and music were written. It is sung at the Communion of the Mass in thanksgiving to God—and widely just now in memory of Napoleon. Born *two hundred years ago.*"

The emphasis, "two hundred years," was slight but apparent. He was smiling now. "But then, Corsicans have always found much to sing about."

He helped himself to more of the small, bright raspberries and extended the bowl to me. "It does occur to me, however, that one might reasonably *rephrase* your question. One might ask, for example, how our Corsican hymn of victory reached your United States? . . . Through the ears of an appreciative American visitor to our shores? Or, perhaps, the energies of a traveling young composer who, once back home, found the words and tempo for a different pride, on a different plane of time? . . . Though apparently, as you indicate, *not before 1769.*"

The numerals exploded in my mind . . . 1769! Stephen Foster would not have been born. The fruit bowl still hovered between us, waiting for my belated grasp of it.

"Thank you," I said, taking hold, though I *might* as well have been clutching a small bomb. I stared vacantly at the berries.

"They are a little overripe, I'm afraid," Father Zerga cautioned. "Sugar helps. Otherwise, if you don't know better, they can sometimes make for bitter swallowing."

His laugh was warm. I remember it still. But somehow I think Father Zerga reflects more comfortably on our time together than I do.

That afternoon, thanks to Father Zerga's detective work, I boarded the bus that indeed was under the stewardship of the Bastia rental agency's *clerk's sister's godfather,* Damiano, for the drive to the terminus of his route . . . Bonifacio, identified in a tourist brochure as "perhaps the strangest town in the Mediterranean—an imposing citadel compressed onto a narrow limestone strip overlooking the sea and facing Sardinia." The brochure also heralded its "practically impregnable" status.

It was ten o'clock at night by the time I was led to the second floor of Damiano's home to one of the unadvertised rooms available to friends of his obviously extended family. The single bed was one of four, distributed in a chain of rooms that ran north-south, separated by what may once have been sliding doors but now devoid of them. A sleeping gentleman occupied each of the three, through which Damiano confidently moved, flashlight in hand, to the sequential sleep-sounds of heavy breathing, snoring, and—adjacent to mine—a soft, throaty whistle.

I was not to worry about waking my neighbors. My 40-watt bed lamp was turned on "until you can get out of your things." Mine was the choice room, Damiano confided, with a view of the sea. I was tired enough to sleep on a rock. And, in fading consciousness, the sounds of togetherness evoked the redolent body warmth of summer camp dormitories.

I woke to a room of sunshine. A wispy-thin curtain veiled a multipaned sliding door of glass. It was eight o'clock. I'd slept almost ten hours. On the foot of my bed were the clothes in which I'd arrived and now I climbed hurriedly back into them. Little by little—with utmost care—I determined I was alone in the four-room expanse. I headed back for my bag, but first I wanted that "view of the sea." The windows needed washing but slid easily apart and I stepped out onto a tilted balcony, a string mop on a hook to the left of me, and a half-missing board where I had planned to put my right foot.

The breath went out of me, and my hands flung out flat against the stucco walls. About 200 feet below was the sea, above which seagulls showed their backs, having apparently reached maximum flight altitude. Beneath me, I told myself, must surely lie some segment of the limestone cliff on which I survived the night, though I could not see it. Royal blue water was making craters of white foam against rocks . . . far . . . far below.

When I checked out, Mrs. Damiano collected the modest cost of the room, which she confessed was the most expensive because of its "terrace."

At noon I was put on a bus to Ajaccio on Corsica's western coast, like some continuing parcel-post delivery. I had a note from Damiano's wife to her *sister-in-law's nephew*, who managed a hotel there. Since I was coming "from family," they would find a place for me in one of the gabled rooms that were otherwise limited to staff occupancy.

Ajaccio, the country's capital and the last stop on my Corsican triad, vastly enlarged my bonding with Napoleon: this time in the unlikely context of my encounter with a local aficionado of American songs. More accurately, the aficionado of a particular American singer.

The hotelkeeper in Ajaccio housed me for the three days it took him—through familial connections—to negotiate a plane ticket: Ajaccio-Nice-Paris-San Francisco. Appreciatively I packed in for him several bottles of the best wine I could find—a meager gesture, given the enormity of his accomplishment. But what really enchanted him was my willingness to visit and report to him my impressions of the capital's Napoleonic landmarks.

He had a list.

My first sortie was to the small ancestral home of the Bonaparte family, identified as "full of the atmosphere of Corsica, in which simplicity and austerity are inextricably mingled with grandeur and legend," followed by the Palace of Cardinal Fesch (the priestly uncle of Napoleon who was to crown him in Notre Dame, Paris) and the Monument to the Emperor (the work of Seurre le Jeune).

After day two I checked off my landlord's list Napoleon's Baptistery, the Grotto in which he is said to have played as a child, and the written memorabilia on display at the "Library."

By day three Napoleon was wearing very thin. The magic of Corsica, for me, lay in its compelling land and its people. Ajaccio, a town of white houses spread along the foothills of a mountain-fringed gulf, drew me to the outdoors like metal to a magnet. After a conscience-clearing run through the home of the woman who had embroidered some of the Confirmation attire of the boy Napoleon (to which accomplishment a brass plaque beside the front door attested), I took to the fresh air on one of the long café terraces.

The man at a table beside me was drinking a *pastis*, that licorice-tasting drink widely favored in much of the western Mediterranean. I ordered one. The addition of water to the concentrated yellow-green pastis turns it instantly cloudy. I'd forgotten, and gave a little sound of surprise.

"C'est normal!" The man at the next table was laughing. I had made my tourist status evident, and when I identified myself as from the United States, his eyes grew wide in delight.

"The home of Jeannette MacDonald!"[3]

He stood up, reached out and gripped both my hands, shaking them with a kind of congratulatory zeal. "A great privilege . . . Jeannette MacDonald," repeating her name with the reverent wonder that I—a living link to her—was actually there in front of him.

"*Rosemarie, Maytime, Sweethearts, New Moon . . .*" The list of her many films went on. "With a voice that put the birds to shame and so beautiful . . . beautiful."

I smiled my agreement.

"And red hair. I have never seen such color."

I struggled to make some contribution. "It was real, you know," I said. "The same off-screen."

"You knew her?"

"I met her in California. I was . . ."

His hand had gone to my wrist, and the rest of the sentence was aborted as together we sailed into the modest restaurant bar. There he released his grip, and his arms went out expansively.

"Everybody! I would like you to meet my lady from America and a friend of Jeannette MacDonald!" 'Jeannette' was stretched into three dramatic syllables.

Actually I had "met" Jeannette MacDonald as guest of a part-time usher and voice student whom I briefly dated when I was in junior high school. The occasion was a concert in which she was featured with the San Francisco Symphony. Backstage after the concert, she had given him her autograph, nodded to me, and shook my hand. Never had I anticipated that the product of those few seconds would bring me mercurial fame in a Corsican city.

"Jojo" was the name of her passionate Corsican enthusiast, but she was not unappreciated by Jojo's friends at the bar.

I began again. "I just wanted to say that I met Jeannette MacDonald in San Francisco . . ."

"In '*San Francisco*'!" the bartender said. "I saw that film. Nelson Eddy wasn't in that one, was he?"

"Clark Gable . . . I think," I interjected. "A movie about the earthquake."

"You're right!" Jojo pointed a triumphant finger. "But she sang. Sure she sang *that* song: 'San Francisco.'" He was looking at me for confirmation.

"Well, yes." I was digging myself in deeper with each effort.

Jojo ordered a round of drinks. We all toasted Jeannette MacDonald, and with the second sip the faces turned as one toward me as Jojo intoned, with a newfound solemnity: "And to her faithful friend from America." He was waiting for my name. I gave it, and he added it to the shared Salut!

By now there was no unraveling anything. I simply nodded in endorsement of all dimensions of praise. Jojo had seen seven of her films. *Maytime* was his favorite. For Jojo, the United States—whatever his broader knowledge of it—had dominant reality as a culture in the emotionally charged backdrop of MGM musicals.

The bartender was setting up a third round of drinks, with whose consumption I had failed to keep up. I was planning my exit line when Jojo, reading my mind, spoke again. "A last drink, to her memory."

We toasted. I tried fruitlessly to pay. "I must go. I have a plane to catch this afternoon."

That announcement generated a shift in Jojo's concentration. "You have, of course, seen our treasures of Napoleon."

I rattled off the significant number that I had run up.

" . . . and The Napoleon Museum in the Hotel de Ville," Jojo finished.

"Next time," I assured him. "It is closed today."

"But you cannot leave without seeing the very best on the island, the museum collection." His hand went to his pocket. "I have the key. *I am the Assistant Curator.*"

"There is no time, Jojo."

"Nowhere in Ajaccio . . . nowhere in the world can you ever again see these things. Paintings, furniture, jewelry . . . the CROWN!" His friends were closing in, nodding agreement.

"What is the time of your flight?" someone asked.

"Five-thirty to Nice. With a tight connection to Paris."

"There is a city van in the museum lot. Do not worry. With that I can drive you right onto the field if we need to." He took a look at my stricken face. "But we will not have to."

In ten minutes he had opened the Napoleon Museum in the Hotel de Ville and we walked through the impressive collection. A guided tour. Just for me, Jeannette MacDonald's friend.

At the airport Jojo double-parked his city van and walked me to the gate.

"You will make your connection at Nice . . . trust me," he said. From his pocket he took out one of the large, round lapel pins (with the bust of Napoleon in gala military dress) that I had seen among the mementos on sale at the museum. I was touched and thanked him.

"No! No!" he said as I started to open my purse. "Wear it. As a favor to me. Please, do not take it off until you are in Paris, okay?"

The "okay" was in English, and I laughed my promise. A funny fellow. I'd be trailing images of Napoleon, literally, into France's capital. I was the last to board, waving my good-bye. The memories were good ones.

But as we circled Nice, delayed in our clearance to land, the joy seeped out of me. Odds of my making the Nice flight to Paris were dwindling, and I had run out of Corsican "emergency-staff relatives" to move me along the supercrowded airways.

We landed on a field flirting with darkness. A bus, we were told, would be needed to take us to the terminal, and we must wait for it. And *that* I decided was the death knell for my getting a boarding pass and for any illusions about my connection to Paris.

I joined the passengers deplaning down a mobile, metal staircase that had been pushed alongside. It was glaringly illuminated.

"Madame Anderson?"

I was on the airstrip. The voice came from behind the bright lights, I nodded, and someone took hold of my arm. We moved a yard or two away, and I found myself beside a black-jacketed man with a helmet.

"Do not be afraid. Jojo told me how to find you." He tapped my lapel-pin bust of Napoleon. "I have the flight information. I will get you to the plane."

He led me to a motorcycle a few yards away as the rest of the passengers streamed out of sight. After some coaching I straddled the rear of the motorcycle seat and the man squeezed my small suitcase in front of him.

"Wrap your arms around my waist and hang on," he instructed. "There is no danger so long as you hang on."

It wasn't far, but it was fast. And there we were alongside another plane, the Nice-Paris plane. I could see the profiles of passengers in the lighted interior. Outside, another flight of metal stairs still pressed against the body of the plane.

"Will he wait for us?" I cried out.

"Oh, I think so," came from the driver. "He's expecting us."

"He *is*?"

"Oh yes. I phoned him . . . he's my *brother-in-law, my sister's husband*."

We had stopped. He took off his helmet and put the suitcase in my hand as I got off.

"And who are *you*?" I yelled over the noise of the plane.

"Jean-Paul . . . Jojo's my *brother*," the voice roared back. "Didn't the idiot tell you?"

Someone grabbed my suitcase and guided me to the plane. When I turned at the top of the stairs, Jean-Paul was waving and with my free hand I waved back.

Notes

[1] Alan Lomax, "The Cultural Context of Folk Songs," in Walter Goldschmidt, *Exploring the Ways of Mankind* (2d ed.) (New York: Holt, Rinehart and Winston, 1971), 600–614.

[2] "Swanee River"'s correct title is "Old Folks at Home" (published in 1851). The *Suwannee* River is located in Georgia.

[3] Recalling Jeannette MacDonald was a challenge. The singing duo of Jeannette MacDonald and Nelson Eddy drew avid theater audiences of the 1930's films whose plots were contrived to feature their joint and separate vocal talents—often with impressive off-camera orchestral accompaniment. Jeannette MacDonald later made occasional appearances on concert stages. Reruns of their movies appeared. And at least one TV special featured memorable highlights.

THE
CHALLENGE
OF CHANGE

10

Megacultures
The Politics of Control in China and Russia

Each field experience takes on a mystique of its own: a coalescence of parts into distinctive wholeness. The anthropologist struggles to make sense of fragments of culture and their sometimes masked or reticent contribution to a unique formula for living.

China would prove a megachallenge: a country within which more than one billion men, women, and children put twenty-four hours of daily living behind them. Experiencing China leaves one searching for adjectives with which to convey the wrap-around, teeming, 3-D, Technicolor reality of life within it. Yet from the start, however incongruously, there was communicated an unmistakable sense of overriding, synthesizing, ordered control. The country cannot be understood apart from this dominance of "control."

For the village-honed anthropologist, China is not an easy transition. And if the field assignment includes applied work and pan-China commitments, the humblest of goals take on new meaning.

The former Union of Soviet Socialist Republics was also daunting.[1] By the mid-1980s, internal regional tugs and threats to its "wholeness," however defined, were already evident. As the largest country on earth it spanned eleven time zones. *Eleven*. That meant that when it was noon in captive Lithuania, midnight had already descended upon the family beside the bone-chilling Gulf of Anadyr on the Bering Sea. The Russian-dominated U.S.S.R. occupied one-half of the world's northern hemisphere. Its people spoke over 100 different languages.

Small wonder Russia had problems keeping all this terrain appreciative of its leadership and its flag. The government-ascribed unity fooled no one. Culturally the U.S.S.R. functioned as a disturbing hybrid: a world of frenetic calm. Winston Churchill called it "a riddle wrapped in mystery inside an enigma." For Russia itself, a single word comes to mind. Russia *endures*.

Neither China nor Russia has ever left much to goodwill in terms of control of its wide-ranging peoples, as I would learn when I found myself successively a guest of both countries: in 1982 visiting China's specialists in gerontology and geriatric medicine and two years later working with the Soviet Medical Workers Union hospital- and health-planning personnel. As a member of small U.S. teams (10 of us in China; 12 in the U.S.S.R.) I traveled widely, covering thousands of miles in each country.

The modest grant-declared goals of the programs were essentially the same—that we learn from their specialists and they, in turn, profit from our teams' combined experience in areas that both host countries had stated relevant to effecting optimal change in some of their existing patterns of care. This projected democratic exchange, however, never materialized.

In China the proposed interpersonal dynamics, along with the project's goals, were redesigned. Interaction proved almost immediately on an ill-balanced course. China's specialists very much wished to know what we knew about the care of older populations well and sick but intended to keep us on a very short leash in terms of hands-on research. Efforts to engage health personnel in open discussions, debate, or speculation on the pros and cons of existing or proposed programs were avoided or aborted. We were heavily programmed for "model" achievements in almost every aspect of Chinese life. At one "typical" farm to which we were escorted, the oxen had bright new ribbons tied to their horns.

Russia, our host in the U.S.S.R., would essentially prove committed to what might also be called a "display posture," rooted in the conviction that only the laudable (or what could be made laudable) in its practices and facilities should be the stuff of our daily agenda. The source of this posture lay in the soon evident but unexpressed belief that our government-sponsored team was in their country for the less than creditable purpose of ferreting out deficiencies in care.

In both countries, deciphering the subtleties of "indirection" took valuable time. Developing antennae sensitive to an atmosphere within which "real," unscrambled communication can take place rapidly becomes a critical art. The early days in both countries were feeling-one's-way time. Confrontation, we knew, would be useless.

Neither China nor Russia wanted us wandering about alone.

Both provided "facilitators"; in China, with one exception, they were men and in the U.S.S.R., more often women. Their range of comfort with English varied widely. All were programmed: (1) to prepare us for what we were about to experience, (2) tell us what we were experiencing, and finally (3) explain its relevance in terms of their translation of our mission. In China an additional step inevitably subsumed the lengthy and elaborate presentation of our team to supervisory personnel (often considerable) of whatever university, institute, hospital, agency, commune or home for the aged we were about to visit or with whom we were about to work. The *manifest* script was one of revelation: what we knew, what they knew; what we did, what they did. Indeed great time, effort, and assistance were more often than not graciously accorded us by many people. At the same time, increasingly evident were the rehearsed dimension of our activities and the fastidious tracking of us.

In both countries a major mechanism for the latter goal was what might be called "saturation programming." Our daily schedule had no holes. From breakfast to an unverbalized but virtual curfew, we followed 'the schedule' for the day . . . one that allowed rare deviations and restricted our movements to predetermined itineraries.

Our Chinese and Russian colleagues were fiercely interested in whatever knowledge and experience we might bring to issues on which they sought insight or simply on data to which they had limited access. But they remained overridingly cautious in eliciting formal exchange. Short of independent initiative on our part, the world we would see would largely be the cultural world China and Russia had programmed for us to see.

Yet, in many places, particularly the more isolated villages and towns of China, there was no way in the world that governments could insulate us from contact with local people, many of whom had never before set eyes on a Westerner. Passersby were courteous but avidly curious. Often men and women and children walked along beside us in small tides, staring and talking animatedly among themselves, matching our strides, pouring into stores we sometimes simply chose to enter. Timid, they always managed to leave us breathing space. At these times, I would feel something like the yolk of an egg, cushioned with only a trickle of space from an encompassing shell. And there was a disturbing sense of the same fragility.

On one occasion when our guide had rather oversold the purported inventory of a local department store (not the usual Friendship Store reserved for outsiders and privileged party members), a Chinese onlooker intervened as I chose to buy one of the simple, widely worn, cotton tunics. To the delight of the crowd around me I had tried it on and was in the process of paying for it when an elderly woman surged forward and angrily confronted the clerk. A wild, incomprehensible debate followed between them. But the woman was firm and despite the clerk's protestations unfolded the tunic and put it on me again. With brisk tugs and shakes of her head she made clear that only a smaller size would do justice to the appropriate fit. Her rapid Chinese never faltered as her eyes locked on mine.

I didn't *want* a smaller size. But when I conveyed as much, there was near-pandemonium as the crowd began to take sides. Finally, I raised my arms above my head and called out one of the few words that came to mind from my pre-trip, eight-week crash course in Chinese: "Stop!" Then I dredged up the word for "Two!" and held two fingers high above my head as I helped myself to the second, smaller tunic in the woman's hands. . . . In broad pantomime and corrupt Chinese, I conveyed that I would buy *both* tunics, a resolution that seemed to meet with resounding approval from the crowd and a great smile from my fashion counselor, who now supervised payment in a careful selection of money from my outstretched wallet, as two tunics were folded into the flimsy store bag. Then, before there could be any major regrouping, I made my swift way back into the streets.

On Russian streets, even remote ones, we were less a novelty. But getting to know people as individuals was not easy. Our moving about routinely as a "pack" was a pall on communication. Once in a while when we piled up, negotiating access to a subway or bus, we'd manage brief exchanges. In interpersonal contacts, the Russians were bolder than the Chinese.

A standard report, among us, was of men and women taking the initiative and, in halting English, checking us out as a possible resource for *blue jeans*. Russians were wild to have them. Wear them. Or, apparently, to spend whatever sum of money it took for black-market rerouting of them. We speculated that an enterprising (and brave) traveler could write off the cost of a trip to Russia if he or she could get a suitcase full of blue jeans through customs. One creative young man had an extra pair of local trousers folded into his jacket for a strip exchange.

The best way to negotiate independent roaming was to plead interest in seeing all we could of the country's rich heritage: vestiges of a glorious past or marvels of the present. In the stunning city of (then) Leningrad we had no problem with our expressed desire to roam its canals and bridges. . . . And if we sometimes wandered off, there were more apologies than repercussions.

More worrisome were the overtures of individuals who in China and in Russia occasionally sought out some of us clandestinely, usually on the rare occasions when we were billeted not in the pseudo-European hotels expressly prepared for "outsiders," but in the mixed-housing arrangements in both countries' bulging cities.

In one sprawling new Shanghai complex into which we were absorbed, the uninvited guest was a woman I found in my room on our return from an exquisite but long and mysterious Chinese opera.

I had the room to myself, a welcome change from our usual constraints. The overhead fixture didn't work and before fully closing the door, I groped beside my bed for the night stand's incongruous art-deco lamp with its red and black shade. As light flooded the area, I saw a woman seated on a chair alongside the prominent (and prized) TV set with its velvet dust cover. She put her fingers to her lips, and I walked over and closed the door. I hadn't cried out and that was fortunate, but I was shaken.

What I would learn over the next hour was the story of an aborted medical career that left her not the physician she had wanted all her life to be and had been close to becoming, but a simple medical aide in a ward on the city's outskirts. Now, little more than a decade beyond China's devastating Cultural Revolution, which vigorously opposed the creation or existence of professional elites and—as she now graphically recounted—made a bloodbath of established university departments, she remained one of many intellectual casualties. Despite these indictments she was eager to recount the eventual triumph of China's educational systems and what she identified as the "famous class of '77," which reinitiated a cadre of physicians "unmatched in China's long history." In a continuing combination of rage and pride, she let me know that there still lurked the very real risk of being sent to China-dominated Tibet or Inner Mongolia, regardless of one's level of prestige.

Her English, which she had learned as a child from missionaries, was excellent, and I told her so. I was trying, at the same time, to introduce something cordial and supportive, as a transition from the confessional nature of what had largely amounted to a monologue and which (beyond the privacy of a room I hoped was unbugged) would have proved politically dangerous in the extreme.

At last she stood up, and so did I. She was smiling. "It was good to talk."

I had my hand on the doorknob, turned it, and checked the hall. "Can you find your way out all right?" I found myself troubled for her.

"There must always be a way out," she said. And I watched until she disappeared down the staircase.

We did see much of China by plane, bus, car, and battered taxi. In the minds of a few of our ever-changing Chinese colleagues and guides, my identification with medical anthropology was once again synonymous with "physician," so that I was sometimes diverted from a hospital tour to its surgical-viewing theater and once actually found myself scrubbing up to share a privileged view of chest surgery performed with the use of acupuncture in place of Western methods of anesthesia. Almost as memorable was the visibility, within many hospitals, of Chinese families involved in the care and comfort of relatives. Often they brought and prepared food in the sick room or replaced bed linens from home. Sometimes they took the night watch over a patient needing extended supervision. The rooms still managed to look orderly and clean, if not fastidious. This familial involvement seemed to me an anxiety-reducing feature of Chinese hospital care and cost efficient. The practice was most evident where specialized hospitals were rare and prioritized within the internal hierarchy of communes, their relative size and location.

China was proud of its communes.

We visited many. One of these, in the heavily populated Yangtze Delta, was heralded as a prime representative of China's emerging "responsibility system."

Agricultural activities of the commune of Bei Quiao were carried on by 12 production brigades, which, we were told, jointly subsumed 120 hands-on production teams and one seed farm. Their multiple crops, weather conditions permitting, included wheat, rice, and cotton as well as several vegetables and medicinal herbs. A small commune factory made shaft parts for fabric mills. With factory work paying more than field work, only one person per commune family could work in the factory. Money gained from factory sales was committed to the enhancement of communal mechanization.

The increasing and shifting "initiative" of communes was heralded by each of our several nonlocal guides as a fine-tuning, *not* a surrender, of socialist principles. The state still owned the land; a small amount was given up to individual plots for family profit. A bumper harvest meant family-shared bonuses for everyone.

This was the largest commune we would see and evidently a showplace. Our guide/interpreter was good-natured. He smiled and was intent on our understanding everything, so that he was given to repeating the last words of many sentences whose meaning he thought might otherwise escape us. "After the storeroom we go to the shop . . . the shop." "This is very nice house with small flower garden . . . flower garden." My questions as to the scope of commune versus free-market income brought his first brow-wrinkling display of disappointment. Clearly he was expecting greater appreciation of the "enormous very good changes" in place. Then came the predictable barrage of figures. We were told that with 19,488 people, 5,364 families, and a total labor force of 12,999 "everybody gains . . . gains."

In the afternoon we were programmed to visit the commune's own home for the aged, or "happiness house" as these were sometimes translated for us. But first, lunch was served in a pleasant, simple dining room. The food was good and overplentiful. I counted seventeen service plates. As usual the meal was preceded by a brief welcoming speech, this time by Mr. Liu, commune "head."

Our American team had developed a rotating system of responsibility for responding (after a meal, tour, lecture, or program), conveying our thanks and appreciation. On this occasion, however, our expressed pleasure in the much-awaited visit to "happiness house" proved premature.

We were not to see it, though it took us a while to figure that out. Mr. Liu himself led us back to our van and waved us off, itself a surprise. "Happiness house," we decided, was apparently considerably removed from the commune's center. But as traffic picked up and time passed, we found ourselves looking wonderingly at one another. *How far was it?*

Finally we put the question to our guide, who sat up in front beside the driver.

The reply was prompt.

"Visiting is not possible today. Very, very sorry."

"What do you mean 'not possible'?" came from someone after a few seconds of stunned surprise.

We had *come* to the commune to visit their accommodations for the elderly. At lunch, when the commune's leaders would surely have been in a position to explain, not a word had been offered of the change in plans.

Ten brains were now searching out some rationale: a special holiday, an outbreak of dengue fever, mud slides? But no expression of chagrin or dismay moved our guide to go beyond his initial declaration, except to repeat it with apparently the best he could do in the way of a qualifier.

"Visiting is not possible today. Maybe soon."

However, over the weeks we would see much of institutional care of China's aged in rural and urban contexts. Some of these showed emulable formulas for incorporating men and women actively in the ongoing life of the communities in which they had spent their lives. Board and lodging, adequate clothing, and the assurance of a proper funeral were among the expressed governmental guarantees.

We learned not to argue with the repeated but absurd script that institutional care for the aged essentially accommodated only those uncommon men and women who had outlived a supportive family.

I suspect our government guides and specialists would have been happier *believing* this to be true. But the aged themselves made clear to us that an overwhelming number of them had living children. Everywhere they took pains to show us photographs of them.

China's mounting challenges to adequate gerontological care centers, we were all aware, lay in the growing social assaults on traditional formulas of family accommodation of aging parents or grandparents, though recent laws had tightened children's responsibilities. Everywhere we found squeezed living space, new two-career young marrieds, and a population explosion that had spawned the controversial one-child-per-family birth control program then newly in effect. These and other factors were devastating old priorities. What was often painfully conceded by Chinese university colleagues (our best source of information) was that China's spiraling rate of growth was generating what was essentially a problem in "culture lag." But for "outsiders"—for us, despite our mission—the official message was rarely one of candor.

Sometimes the Chinese themselves had difficulty accepting the messages promoted for consumption. At a teacher's college in central China, a civil affairs administration officer read to us smilingly from a book of statistics on the current status of the aged, while a young student in biomedical technology who sat beside me nudged me periodically—his hand cupped to his mouth.

"Do you *believe* all this?"

From time to time he would shift his weight impatiently, elbow me, and whisper: "Not right! Not true!"

Giant billboards hyped widespread birth control injunctions. In a parking lot in Wuhan, then a terminus of the Yangtze River ferries, I saw a three-story billboard pictorial rendering of the idealized Chinese family. Mother and father, faces beaming, stood with outstretched arms before a single child, about five years of age, in an otherwise empty and spacious room. Golden light bathed the boy. Everyone was smiling. The sparse script was unreadable, but the message was evident: This is what the family could be, ought to be. Nor was it a matter of secrecy that villages that met full compliance with the one-child edict enjoyed special bonuses. As yet unaddressed were thorny long-range cultural consequences for traditional familial practices.

During our months in China a small network of U.S. consulates kept desultory track of us, but did respond with amazing promptness when word was received that a former American academic guest of China had reported for press release, in the United States, a lengthy account of China's sometimes forced third-trimester abortions. Our group was brought in and told to be packed and ready to leave if political reverberations worsened. But nothing happened. We gravitated back into our "schedule" again.

Yet the incident was the first of several that forced examination of the dynamics of fieldwork in a confrontational culture. And the same unwelcome challenge would come again in the Union of Soviet Socialist Republics: how to function productively and ethically as an anthropologist within an ill-defined, essentially predatory government code of conduct. Judgmental postures, traditionally frowned upon in the training of cultural anthropologists, are too often impossible to avoid. The demands on one's energies is vitiating psychologically and intellectually disturbing.

Realistically, the potential for actual physical danger in China or the U.S.S.R. seemed small. Delimitations of travel, constraints of action, the very supervision we deplored nevertheless constituted a largely fail-safe protective force. Despite an occasional dialogue of doom with someone in authority, the gut-level feeling of the teams was that you couldn't get into trouble if you tried.

However, our too-cramped cocoon eventually did invite revolt. Over time—and in rapid succession—would come chagrin, frustration, deep-seated resentment, and eventually a search for a "way out." Some kind of compromise. We needed to be more routinely in touch with a people whose real face was being more than reasonably masked.

Gradually we became expert at pressing our guides for information. In lectures we gave at health facilities and government agencies, we pushed for more involvement with audiences. In academic contexts we invited student response, opening question-and-answer periods. Or, we would drop innocently behind on a hospital tour or on a busy street. We used what we had mastered of the language to engage an occasional merchant or passerby in halting conversation.

In a Chinese nursing home, when the group turned right at a corridor junction, I turned left into a small dormitory. Two women, fully clothed, were sitting on beds. I smiled, offered them each a wrapped chocolate (we carried them principally for children, who delighted in them), and pulled out the two or three photos I always carried with me of my children. One woman went to the wall cupboard and removed a framed family portrait, pointing to a younger image of herself with husband and five children. She identified those who lived nearby and those faraway. The other woman, very old with creased face and hands . . . had *bound feet*, no more than five inches long. I pointed to them. She nodded, laughed her confirmation, and threw back both hands in the clear communication that the outdated practice was taking us back a long, long way in time.[2]

A standard precaution of our mentors was the frequent head count of our ever-moving team, so that we did not fear being seriously stranded. The "lost" member was rescued with sufficient regularity that reverberations were rare.

A more daring resource was what, among ourselves, we called "running away." Running away meant the judicious restructuring of time in line with our own priorities, not our hosts'. Our state-programmed visit to (then) Leningrad's Hermitage Museum excluded its most notable holdings in favor of hours devoted to viewing the "art of the revolution": rooms laden with paintings of rousing battles, banners, and blood. Somewhere within the Hermitage, we knew, were the world-famous acquisitions of Catherine The Great and a World War II bounty of Impressionist paintings. We might never again have the opportunity to see them! Indeed, the so-near-and-yet-so-far effect was so powerful that a propitious "sore-throat epidemic" swept our little group, as a consequence of which several of us (serially) missed the tour of yet another monument or new dam or sewage system. And we revisited the Hermitage. None of us invited risk-taking *for its own sake*, but motivation sometimes took hold when one cared enough about some thing, some event, some defensible opportunity that anything less than exploring it was more than reason could condone. But these undertakings were rare.

The Russians took a more sober stance on our camera use than did the Chinese. During one orientation session shortly after our arrival in Ukraine and the inevitable check of our identification documents, we were reminded of local limitations on taking photos. Three restrictions were emphasized.

(These seemed to change with each republic.) We were not to take pictures of airports nor of tunnels nor of any Ukrainian without first asking permission. "Airport" made sense. I could not imagine why any of us would want to venture into a tunnel. The third was not a problem either. It was common courtesy.

The season, I remember, was one in which flower stands were bursting with gladiolas. Gladiolas of red, yellow, orange were everywhere. Local women congregated at makeshift stands selling them in great bunches. These were scenes *meant* for picture taking. So I asked, and to my surprise the women nervously refused.

Later that day, having gone out to mail a couple of postcards, I looked over the rim of a hillside street and saw, in an open-air market below me, a whole enclave of gladiola vendors. To solicit permission was impossible. They were too far away. I waved anyway. . . several times. But no one had any reason to be looking up—or even aware of me. I took out my camera and made the shot. Then a second one from a different angle.

As I turned away and took perhaps ten steps, two men moved in front of me. They wore dark suits and, although the day was warm, lightweight black topcoats. To my surprise one of them extended his hand across the yard or two between us. He wanted my camera. With a second gesture he showed that he intended to pull my film from it.

My first reaction was that this was some insane kind of holdup. But together they persisted in blocking my passage.

"KGB," someone insisted later. But I hadn't a clue. Then the hand went out again for my camera. With serious intent.

To this day I have no real explanation for what I did. Nor do I regard it as anything an intelligent, reflective anthropologist, or anyone, ought to do. But my reaction was automatic.

"No way!" I said, waving a hand in indignation as I thrust myself forward between them, the camera clasped protectively to my chest. I walked on and I didn't look back.

It was only seconds before the insanity of my action really hit me, and I mentally braced myself for what must surely follow. Minimally my arrest. But, miraculously, nothing did, and I steeled myself to keep walking, and not look back.

Once in a while the experience comes vividly to mind, especially when I am trying to convey what can happen to one's innate sense of reason and professionalism in the face of what one sees as the "unreasonable" worlds of controlled cultures.

The China and U.S.S.R. experiences were rewarding, largely in ways I had not expected. Applied anthropology, the contracted commitment to function as an agent of change, involves problems and ethical issues for which we *will not be ready*. Training is critical, experience priceless.

Most of us have painfully learned that—anywhere in the world—understanding must be accommodated, not only within the logic that molds another country's culture (or cultures), but simultaneously within the just-as-durable logic and behavioral codes that shape the priorities and motivation of the anthropologist. Resistance, wherever it occurs, whatever the dynamics, is by definition a two-party product.

Good fieldwork involves a readiness to develop new "antennae" for making sense of the culture within which we have committed ourselves to work. Formulae for getting those antennae "out there" with unslanted vision vary with the terrain. Every time. With practice we get better at it. But the job is never easy, never flawless.

The most we hope for is our best prepared effort. And most of the time we find enjoyment and growth in the challenges.

Notes

[1] "Soviet," *Webster's New World Dictionary* tells us, means a council or body of delegates: "in the Soviet Union, any of the various governing councils, local, intermediate, and national, elected by and representing

the people: they constitute a pyramidal governmental structure, with the village and town Soviets at its base and the Supreme Soviet as its apex."

[2] From Joyce McCarl Nielsen, 1990. *Sex and Gender in Society: Perspectives on Strategy* (2nd ed.) (Prospect Heights, IL: Waveland Press, 1990), 43.

Footbinding is a custom practiced in China beginning around A.D. 1000 and continuing into the early twentieth century. It involves binding the feet of young girls (three to five years old, depending on the family's social status) in order to restrict their growth. As part of the process, the four smaller toes are bent underneath the foot; this causes the bones to break and the toes to atrophy, both of which are extremely painful.

Although the practice is said to have originated by an emperor's admiration of a dancer's small feet, it took root and became normative in a period of increasing control of women's behavior. The goal for upper-class girls was a three-inch foot; for others it was four to five inches. The effect of having bound feet, of course, was decreased mobility and in many cases an inability to walk at all. The practice was less prevalent in southern China, where women's labor was required in the rice fields, but 50 to 80 percent of all Chinese women are estimated to have had bound feet in the nineteenth century.

Epilogue

In one of those unheralded little events that forever color one's thinking, I learned while listening to my car radio of a secretary in Florida who had a phenomenal memory for voices. Heard once, a voice took on such distinctiveness—in whatever cerebral receptors influence such recall—that she could, after a lapse of as much as five years, identify the caller by name.

I should think she would be paid as handsomely as the company vice-president. Imagine the sales impact.

"Hello, Mr. Jefferson. My goodness, it's been a long time, hasn't it? I'm sure Mr. Garfield will want to know you're on the line. Would you hold for just one moment, please."

And she was not secretive in relaying the source of her awesome powers. For this woman, voices have color and texture. Mr. Jefferson, for example, had "a crumbly yellow voice." Unmistakable. The imagery lay slotted away in her mind like a slide, speedily identifiable when the need for projection arose.

My "receptors" do not work that way at all. Familiar voices bounce off the walls of my mind elusive as a tennis bell. What I realized some years ago, however, is that I seem rarely to forget a *smell*. That sickening sweetness of natural gas, for example, transports me in seconds to the tiny Danish kitchen where, in fleece-lined boots and a dyed lamb jacket, I cooked meals for three on a leaky two-plate burner through a brutish Danish winter. When the man came to put grasspaper in the study of my home, the first whiff of wallpaper paste and I was back in France, interviewing Louise in the room where a warm sun baked peeling walls. And there are happy odors. Lilies of the valley and it's May Day in Paris. A fragrant yellow rose and I'm in a Moroccan marketplace scooping up armloads of them at forty cents a dozen. The smell of teak and I can see the wood dust shimmering in the filtered sunlight of the forests of north India, where great elephants gathered the fallen teak logs, obedient to the commands of mahouts who match the rhythm of their bodies to the slow precision of the animal's, riding with an intimate, demanding pride.

Over the years I have come to appreciate the claims that fieldwork inevitably makes on mind and body in forging an appreciation of, and identification with, another culture . . . and often in new reflections on one's own. We search for the intellectual and emotional framework that energizes another population. The day-in-day-out involvement of the field shapes a patchy framework as we acquire data: some of it rich, some of it—initially at least—incomprehensible. The experience is like trying to put together a building, without the blueprints, without some sense of the purpose the structure is intended to serve, the cultural needs it will eventually reflect.

Then, ever so gradually, certain options for the organization of insights begin to suggest themselves as we listen, observe, and participate in the life around us to the extent we can. Sometimes the data we acquire take an unexpected direction, and we find ourselves having to rethink the questions we've been asking: always a good sign. It means the data are speaking to us with new authority, pointing directions toward which our energies need a well-tailored nudge. Our field methods do yield more clarity; the daily piles of fieldnotes, greater satisfaction.

The prospect of some real synthesis pumps joy into our hearts and minds. We handle setbacks with more aplomb. We have kinder thoughts about whatever population has been so demonstrably cavalier about the outcome of our research. And, with a keener sense of the issues that confront us, we find ourselves readier for effective work.

But whatever the course and however committed or fortunate the fieldworker, progress in the field is as often backward as forward, as much blind luck as wisdom, more spasmodic than measured . . . and best sustained by a sense for the comic. For, however galling, it is useful to realize that very often we learn as much from our failures as from our successes—as the chapters of this book must surely have demonstrated. Morocco or China, Russia or France (or in the relative predictability of our own cultural backyard), the "field" is always bumpy terrain. In the field one learns to delight in the small successes, roll with the frustrations, and never keep score.

When anthropologists find themselves sharing field stories, the standard direction of recall is not in tales of progress grimly achieved, but of experiences from which we may well have learned but that—retrospectively, at least—make for laughter. Often these are etched in memory because in one way or another we found ourselves "one-upped" by a cultural situation, usually simple in the extreme for the "natives," in which we performed on a scale from bad to abysmal. And, most often, the roots of our problems lay in the unappreciated fact that a good deal more than diligent brainwork (however valued) was involved. For, in the field, brain *and* body must make cultural adaptations. Ideally it's a joint operation, but the body seems always to retain veto power and sometimes exercises it.

Take the simple and universal act of "gesturing." The world's cultures are riddled with distinctive gesture-systems. These are often tricky to "translate." Some very nearly defy replication on the part of the outsider.

After almost two months in India, for example, I still struggled ineffectively to replicate a not uncommon "head gesture." Visibly it appeared easy enough. The head bobs neither up-and-down (as in the conventional "Yes" of agreement), nor does it move categorically right-to-left/left-to-right (in the communication of "No" or disagreement). The Indian head maneuver was essentially *circular*. And I couldn't do it. The head rotation was so physically alien that, in occasional pockets of time—when no one was looking—I found myself spending time in front of a mirror trying to execute it. Appropriate use of it, I told myself, would have considerable utility, conveying as it did a kind of reticence to accept what was being said, of not exactly going along with what was being proposed, but not an outright rejection of it. Actually what was involved in taking on the head-gesture-challenge was a *double cultural mastery*: (1) being able to perform it well enough for its meaning to be understood and (2) knowing when to use it. Body and mind required a new culturally relevant synchronization, something I was never able to accomplish with expectable Indian grace.

But I persisted. When, at last, I ventured to include it, however imperfectly, within a social context that seemed really to invite its use, I measured success by anything short of terminating the conversation. It was like getting a "C" on a midterm examination. Not all one hopes for, but still on board.

"Reality" itself is always up for grabs in the field. Defining its shifting boundaries is never anything for which we are fully prepared.

Sometimes the interplay of cultural realities experienced by anthropologists in the context of protracted absences and repeated sorties is most readily revealed when field assignments are behind us, and we return to our homes—and to the sudden awareness of the *unfamiliarity* that the *familiar* has taken on in our absence.

However many the field trips, one seems never immune from the impact of "home." And sometimes it is the most mundane expectation that reminds us how minutely all of us are programmed for a soothing predictability within our own cultural landscape. Sometimes, if we can't find it, we invent it.

After a three-year absence from the United States (my longest), I found myself marveling that the airport at which we were landing was adjacent—dangerously so, I thought—to one of the largest new-car lots I'd ever set eyes on. Not until I stood curbside, waiting for the ride that would take me home, did I realize that what I had been staring at was the airport parking lot. People were driving around in those "new" cars and—in my absence—standards of what constituted handsomeness and design and even color had remarkably altered. My old car had suddenly gotten a lot older. Somehow it didn't seem quite fair.

Jet lag sandbags us all at one time or another. And our senses can run into real adaptional problems even after brief trips. After less than a month at a conference in England where left-lane driving is the rule, I returned to Dallas and two days later, after dinner in an unfamiliar restaurant, drove onto the wrong side of a two-lane street. Perhaps it was the night or the alien location of the restaurant, but I remember not having hesitated in recreating a European road prescription. It took a serene three blocks of driving before the glare of headlights of an oncoming car and the horn of a terrified American driver very rapidly reprogrammed me.

There is no way to sum up whatever it is I have been about in this book's too-limited review of cultures whose complexity and integrity deserve more scrupulous treatment of them. But I have, for the most part, been purposefully discriminate, focusing on field experiences that show the cultural anthropologist at work.

The role of fieldwork in the metamorphosis of the cultural anthropologist holds great interest for me. For the embryonic anthropologist, the "field" completes the classroom, much as the operating theater caps the training and shapes the distinctive gifts of the embryonic surgeon. And over the years, fieldwork continues its contributions as a more or less permanent learning phenomenon.

I believe, too, that we do inevitably, in various ways, find ourselves and—to a surprising extent—our lives reappraised in tandem with our reflection on the peoples and worlds to which we give so liberally of ourselves and wherein we place on the line so much of our identity. And I have no doubt that I have benefitted more from fieldwork than the invaded cultures have from my uncertain tinkering with them.

Fieldwork should not be made saleable as pseudopsychoanalysis. Nor do I propose any inevitable pattern of self, falteringly achieved. Certainly not that fieldwork is consonant with a better or wiser person—or anthropologist. I do believe that it is not merely by election or convention that fieldwork has become the hallmark of our discipline.

Perhaps the real enigma of the field is that in decoding the cultural worlds we enter, we find that we are simultaneously decoding the cultural world we left. A double windfall!

BARBARA GALLATIN ANDERSON is Professor Emeritus of Anthropology at Southern Methodist University where she has held the Chair of University Distinguished Professor. She is author or co-author of seven books—including *First Fieldwork* (also by Waveland Press!). Recipient of numerous fellowships and research awards from the United States and foreign governments, she is currently working in collaboration with the University of Texas Southwestern Medical Center and the Visiting Nurse Association of Dallas on the effects of our growing cultural diversity on existing care-related ethical codes.